THE LURE OF THE LIMERICK

THE LURE OF THE LIMERICK

An Uninhibited History

by

WILLIAM S. BARING-GOULD

Hart-Davis, MacGibbon   LONDON

Granada Publishing Limited
First published in Great Britain
by Rupert Hart-Davis Ltd, 1968

Second impression 1968
Third impression 1969
Fourth impression 1969
Fifth impression 1969
Sixth impression 1969
Seventh impression 1970
Eighth impression 1970

Second edition published in Great Britain 1974
by Hart-Davis, MacGibbon Ltd
Frogmore, St Albans, Hertfordshire, AL2 2NF and
3 Upper James Street, London W1R 4BP

Copyright © 1974 by William S. Baring-Gould

ISBN 0 246 97461 3
Printed in Great Britain
Photo-litho reprint by
W & J Mackay Limited, Chatham from earlier
impression

LIMERICKS

From *A Seizure of Limericks* by Conrad Aiken.
Copyright © 1963, 1964 by Conrad Aiken.
Reprinted by permission of Holt, Rinehart and Winston, Inc.

From the *New York Review of Books*. Copyright © 1966 by W. H. Auden.
Reprinted by permission of Curtis Brown, Ltd.

From *Spilt Milk* by Morris Bishop. Copyright © 1942 by Morris Bishop.
Reprinted by permission of Morris Bishop.

From *The New York Times Book Review*. Copyright © 1965 by Morris Bishop.
Reprinted by permission of Morris Bishop.

From *The Waste Land and Other Poems* by T. S. Eliot.
Reprinted by permission of Harcourt, Brace & World, Inc.

Copyright © 1954 by Edward Gorey. From *The Listing Attic* by Edward Gorey,
by permission of Duell, Sloan & Pearce, affiliate of Meredith Press.

Copyright © 1938 by Ogden Nash. From *Verses From 1929 On* by Ogden Nash,
by permission of Little, Brown and Company.

Copyright © 1961 by Louis Untermeyer. From *Lots of Limericks*
by Louis Untermeyer, by permission of Doubleday and Company. Inc.

THANKS ...

The editor and the publisher would like to thank the following for permission to include in this collection copyrighted limericks and material about the limerick: Conrad Aiken and Holt, Rinehart and Winston, Inc.; W. H. Auden and Curtis Brown, Ltd.; Professor Morris Bishop; Edward Gorey and Duell, Sloan & Pearce, affiliate of Meredith Press; Ogden Nash and Little, Brown and Company, Inc.; Louis Untermeyer and Doubleday and Company, Inc. In compiling a book of limericks many years ago, the late Carolyn Wells wrote that the "true" authorship of the vast majority of limericks is so shrouded in the mists of antiquity that she made little or no attempt to determine authorship. While the editor and the publisher of this volume have taken every care to include all necessary acknowledgments, we offer our sincere apologies to any authors we have inadvertently slighted.

"Limericks are jovial things."
—Norman Douglas

What's Inside

PART ONE:

THE LORE OF THE LIMERICK

I *Apologia:*

"The limerick's an art form complex . . ."

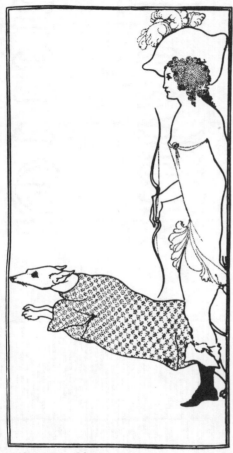

Aubrey Beardsley

THE ULTRAFASTIDIOUS—if such there still be—had best stop reading here: like Phidias, we may startle them:

> There once was a sculptor named Phidias
> Whose manners in art were invidious:
>   He carved Aphrodite
>   Without any nightie,
> Which startled the ultrafastidious

No—this book is not for them.

For surely it is impossible to write of the limerick, its life and high times, without on occasion approaching the indelicate. As the limerick itself has it:

> The limerick's an art form complex
> Whose contents run chiefly to sex;
>   It's famous for virgins
>   And masculine urgin's
> And vulgar erotic effects.

And:

Anon., Idem, Ibid. and Trad.
Wrote much that is morally bad:
    Some ballads, some chanties,
    All poems on panties—
And limericks, too, one must add.

Why, it may be asked, should anyone *want* to write about such an indecorous form of verse as the limerick?

To that question, there are several answers. Probably the best of them is this:

Hardly an *educated* (for the "educated," see Chapter VII) man[1] is now alive who does not treasure in his memory at least one limerick, proper or improper. The chances are that he did not read it in a book or magazine. Rather, he acquired it by hearsay: it was passed on to him by word of mouth, by "oral tradition." As such, the limerick is authentic folklore—a vital part of our heritage.

Said the editors of that short-lived magazine, *Eros,* reporting on the limerick in their fourth and final issue, dated winter, 1962 ("Bawdy Limericks: The Folklore of the Intellectual"):

1. Most women loathe limericks, "for the same reason that calves hate cookbooks," says the erudite and witty folklorist Gershon Legman, who will be spoken of at length later. One of the very few limericks that women seem to appreciate is the following:

For the tenth time, dull Daphnis, said Chloë,
You have told me my bosom is snowy;
    You've made much verse on
    Each part of my person,
Now *do* something—there's a good boy!

André Domin

If you should bump into a serious-looking chap with a note pad on your next visit to a public restroom, do not be alarmed. He is more than likely a member of the American Folklore Society.

The academic community has recently decided that smutty stories and ribald verse are socially significant, and scores of researchers have been turned loose in fraternity smokers, bachelor parties, men's rooms, and other fertile locations to record for posterity the bawdy folklore of A.D. 1963.

And you'll never guess what folkloristic form has emerged as most meaningful—of all things, the limerick!

And yet this normally frivolous and often immoral form of verse can be amazingly high minded at times. The limerick, strangely enough, has been used to instruct and proselytize; to drive home theories physical and metaphysical; to illustrate points in the catechism and other tenets of religion, doctrine and dogma.

Harvey L. Carter, Professor of History at Colorado College, composed this limerick to help students remember the value of *pi:*

'Tis a favorite project of mine
A new value of *pi* to assign.
    I would fix it at 3
    For it's simpler, you see,
Than 3 point 1 4 1 5 9.

The late Professor A. H. Reginald Buller, F.R.S., onetime professor of botany at the University of Manitoba and a world-wide authority on fungi, found time to write many limericks, and not a few of his later years were spent in trying to establish his authorship of a famous verse which first appeared, over his signature, in the English comic weekly, *Punch:*

There was a young lady named Bright
Whose speed was far faster than light;
    She went out one day,
    In a relative way,
And returned the previous night.

"I don't mind the credit going to Bishops, Wits, Established Authors and even that finest of English writers, Anon.," Dr. Buller once complained, "but I do wish they'd get the last line right and preserve the alliteration in the second!" Dr. Buller also wrote a sequel to "Relativity":

> To her friends said the Bright one in chatter,
> "I have learned something new about matter:
>   My speed was so great,
>   Much increased was my weight,
> Yet I failed to become any fatter!"

That puzzling phenomenon, the Fitzgerald contraction, has also been immortalized in a limerick:

> A fencing instructor named Fisk
> In duels was terribly brisk.
>   So fast was his action
>   The Fitzgerald contraction
> Foreshortened his foil to a disk.[2]

Nor should we forget this limerick, by R. J. P. Hewison:

2. Your editor is aware that a bawdy version of this limerick exists. In this case, however—a rare one—we believe that the perfectly proper version came *first*.

A scientist living at Staines
Is searching with infinite pains
    For a new type of sound
    Which he hopes, when it's found,
Will travel much faster than planes.

Modern psychiatry has also been celebrated:

There was a young man from Toledo
Who traveled about incognito;
    The reason he did
    Was to bolster his id
While appeasing his savage libido.

The frustrations of Johnny Carruther
Must stem from this fact and none other:
    There just wasn't room
    To return to the womb,
Occupied, at the time, by his brother.[3]

Word has come down from the Dean
That by use of the teaching machine
    Old Oedipus Rex
    Could have learned about sex
Without ever disturbing the Queen.[4]

3. By J. D. Dunham of Taft, Texas, published in the "Letters" column of *Time,* The Weekly Newsmagazine, March 7, 1935.

4. Published in the *Alumni Review,* Hamilton College, in honor of Fred Skinner, Class of 1926, who as a Harvard professor invented the teaching machine.

One of the most famous of the late Monsignor Ronald Knox's witticisms[5] was a verse built on the Berkleyan idea that things exist only when they have an observer:

> There once was a man who said: "God
> Must think it exceedingly odd
>   If he finds that this tree
>   Continues to be
> When there's no one about in the Quad."

This promptly drew the anonymous reply:

> "Dear Sir, Your astonishment's odd;
> I am always about in the Quad;
>   And that's why the tree
>   Will continue to be
> Since observed by Yours faithfully, God."

Indeed, the Roman Catholic Society of St. Peter and St. Paul has published in both Great Britain and the United States what can only be described

---

5. Knox once persuaded an unwary newspaper editor to run this "classified advertisement":

Evangelical vicar in want of a portable second-hand font, would dispose of the same for a portrait (in frame) of the Bishop-Elect of Vermont.

as a "Limerick Prayer Book," the work of one "G. L. P.," who writes in his preface:

> These rhymes were designed by a priest,
> To affect your religion like yeast;
>   If they help it to grow,
>   Like the yeast in the dough,
> There'll be one better Christian, at least.

Despite all this good work, the limerick, as most of us know it, is aptly described by this anonymous writer:

> The limerick packs laughs anatomical
> Into space that is quite economical.
>   But the good ones I've seen
>   So seldom are clean
> And the clean ones so seldom are comical.

The late Don Marquis voiced much the same thought when he wrote:

Edward Lear

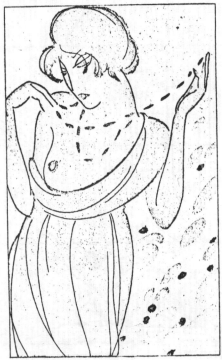

André Domin

It needn't have ribaldry's taint
Or strive to make everyone faint.
    There's a type that's demure
    And perfectly pure
Though it helps quite a lot if it ain't.

And Morris Bishop, one of the great masters of the contemporary limerick, has warned that:

The limerick is furtive and mean;
You must keep her in close quarantine,
    Or she sneaks to the slums
    And promptly becomes
Disorderly, drunk and obscene.

Sofas & bees,
Camels & Keys
Setting a Sneezing & see how
he'll sneeze!

Edward Lear

II *Form:*

"Well, it's partly the shape of the thing . . ."

MUCH OF the charm of the limerick lies in its seductive anatomy.

Professor Francis B. Gummere, writing in *The Popular Ballad,* might well have said of the limerick, as he said of the ballad of tradition: its "differencing quality . . . lies not in its subject, which may be anything, not in its setting, which may be anywhere, but in its actual structure."

And someone else has put this "differencing quality" into the limerick form as:

> Well, it's partly the shape of the thing
> That gives the old limerick wing;
>   These accordian pleats
>   Full of airy conceits
> Take it up like a kite on a string.

Essentially, the limerick is an anecdote in verse.

Its first line sets the scene and introduces the main character; ideally, the rhyme-word at its end is an unusual one:

> *While Titian was mixing rose madder . . .*

The second line rhymes with the first, making a couplet (*a a*). It may introduce a second character and it should open the action which is to precipitate the crisis:

His model reclined on a ladder . . .

The third and fourth lines are shortened to intensify the suspense, and they introduce a new rhyme, hopefully startling, which again make a couplet (*b b*):

Her position to Titian
Suggested coition . . .

The fifth line, enhanced by the end rhyme (*a* again) brings the climax and dénouement of the plot:

So he leapt up the ladder and had 'er.

"There are few poetical forms that can boast the limerick's perfection," Clifton Fadiman wrote in an

André Domin

essay in *Any Number Can Play.* "It has progression, development, variety, speed, climax and high mnemonic value."

And Morris Bishop, in *The New York Times Book Review,* January 3, 1965, wrote: "The structure should be a rise from the commonplace reality of line one to logical madness in line five." And he added with a perfectly straight face: "A scholarly writer in the *Times* [of London] *Literary Supplement* recently pointed out that 'the form is essentially liturgical, corresponding to the underlying ritual of Greek tragedy, with the *parados* of the first line, the *peripeteia* of the second, the *stichomythia* of the two short lines . . . and the *epiphaneia* in the last.' "

In most, but by no means all, limericks, there are usually nine "beats" in lines one, two and five; six "beats" in lines three and four; the third, sixth and ninth "beats" in lines one, two and five are accented: ditty-*dum,* ditty-*dum,* ditty-*dum.*

Scholars call this *anapestic rhythm or foot*—two short syllables and a long; it is the reverse of the *dactyl*—one long (or accented) syllable followed by two short (or unaccented) syllables.[1]

---

1. Neither the *anapest* nor the *dactyl* should be confused with the *trochaic:*

There was a young Scott named McAmiter
Who bragged of excessive diameter;
    Yet it wasn't the size
    That opened their eyes
But the rhythm—trochaic hexameter.

H. I. Brock, in his *Little Book of Limericks*, states that the *paeonic* measure was at one time preferred to the *anapestic* at Yale, and he cites the following limerick as an example of the *paeonic* measure:

> I saw Nelson at the Battle of the Nile,
> And did the bullets whistle—I should smile!
>   And when Pharaoh hit the King
>   With a cutlass on the wing,
> I was lying at the bottom of the pile.

Yale, in our opinion, can have it.

To the poet Leonard Bacon, "the limerick is a specialized form of what used to be called . . . Poulter's Measure. One line contains a dozen syllables and the next fourteen, and both were dear to the hearts of Wyatt and Surrey [Sir Thomas Wyatt, 1503?-1542, and Henry Howard Surrey, by courtesy Earl of Surrey, 1517?-1547], the first poets in modern English."

Queen Elizabeth I, Bacon suggests, *almost* composed a limerick, which you will find in *The Oxford Book of English Verse*:

Aubrey Beardsley

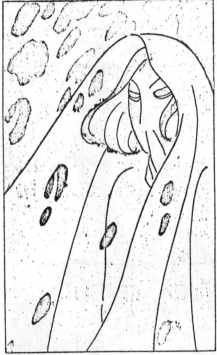

André Domin

The daughter of debate
Who discord aye doth sow,
　　Hath reaped no gain
　　Where former reign
Hath taught still peace to grow.

"Queen Elizabeth is writing Poulter's Measure in [this] stanza," Bacon continues, "but she made the first step toward the formation of a limerick by introducing the interior rhyme in the fourteen syllable line. The next step is to introduce an interior rhyme at the end of the third foot of the twelve-syllable line, when the [limerick] measure may be said to be born."

Certainly the limerick is not a flexible form.

"Now and then," says the poet Louis Untermeyer in his collection *Lots of Limericks,* "some foolhardy experimenter attempts to extend the limerick by altering the shape, adding an extra line. But all such changes destroy the character and compactness of the pure form. To the *aficionado,* there cannot be a six-line limerick any more than there can be a fifteen-line sonnet."

Nonetheless, the late novelist and limerick connoisseur Norman Douglas, about whom we shall have more to say later, was fond of tagging a limerick with a couplet which he thought might make it even more amusing:

> There was a young fellow named Skinner
> Who took a young lady to dinner;
>> At half past nine
>> They sat down to dine,
> And by quarter to ten it was in her.

> *What, dinner?*
> *No, Skinner!*

If the six-line limerick fails to satisfy us, what shall we say of that form of the limerick in which the last line dismally fails to rhyme?

According to G. K. Chesterton, in his essay "Bad Poetry" in *All I Survey,* we can blame this type of limerick on the Reverend Patrick Brontë, father of the Brontë sisters, who once delivered himself of this homily:

André Domin

Religion makes beauty enchanting
And even where beauty is wanting,
    The temper and mind,
    Religion-refined,
Will shine through the veil with sweet lustre.

But Professor T. J. Spencer of Washington, D. C.,
has his own explanation for the origin of this type
of limerick:

The limerick, peculiar to English,
Is a verse form that's hard to extinguish.
    Once Congress in session
    Decreed its suppression
But people got around it by writing the last
    line without any rhyme or meter.

As in:

There was a fat lady from Eye
Who felt she was likely to die;
    But for fear that once dead
    She would not be well-fed,

She gulped down a pig, a cow, a sheep, twelve
    buns, a seven-layer cake, four cups of cof-
    fee, and a green apple pie.

Because the limerick is a self-contained unit,
most limerick *sequences* fail, although many of
them do get off to a good start. An extraordinary
example, running to forty-eight verses, was published in 1943 by Quentin Crisp as *All This and
Bevin Too*. But far and away the best-known of all
limerick sequences was that touched off by a five-
liner which appeared in the *Princeton Tiger* more
than fifty years ago:

There was an old man of Nantucket
Who kept all his cash in a bucket;
    But his daughter, named Nan,
    Ran away with a man,
And as for the bucket, Nantucket.

The Old Man from Nantucket bred many imitations: columnists, their contributors and other college humor magazines competed to supply sequels,
which grew drearier and drearier. Perhaps the best

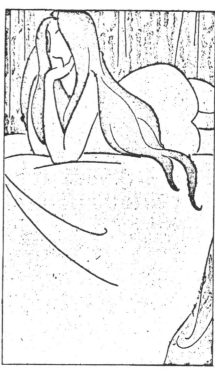

André Domin

2. A noted psychologist, H. J. Eysenck, once tried to establish whether or not the Americans and the British differ in their sense of humor by submitting a group of limericks to representatives of both nations. The Americans chose as the funniest:

> There was a young man of Laconia,
> Whose mother-in-law had pneumonia.
>   He hoped for the worst—
>   And after March first
> They buried her 'neath a begonia.

The British preferred:

> There was a young girl of Asturias,
> Whose temper was frantic and furious.
>   She used to throw eggs
>   At her grandmother's legs—
> A habit unpleasant, but curious.

continuations in the long series were those published by the *Chicago Tribune* and the *New York Press*, respectively:

> Pa followed the pair to Pawtucket
> (The man and the girl with the bucket)
>   And he said to the man,
>   "You're welcome to Nan,"
> But as for the bucket, Pawtucket.

> Then the pair followed Pa to Manhasset,
> Where he still held the cash as an asset;
>   And Nan and the man
>   Stole the money and ran,
> And as for the bucket, Manhasset.

Professor Spencer has noted above that: "The limerick [is] peculiar to English . . . ," and he is quite correct. True, there are quite a few limericks in French kicking up their can-can heels in the compilations (Carolyn Wells included a number of them in her *Nonsense Anthology*), and there are limericks in Latin as well, but, generally speaking, the limerick is an Anglo-American form of verse[2]

—perhaps, as Brander Matthews observed long ago, the *only* original verse form of the English language.

"The limerick loses its quality and its point becomes pointless when it has to be filtered through another language," Louis Untermeyer writes. He cites "a perfectly innocuous limerick" which illustrates the language problem:

There was a young fellow named Hall
Who fell in the spring in the fall.
    'Twould have been a sad thing
    Had he died in the spring,
But he didn't—he died in the fall.

The pun about dying in the spring instead of the fall [Untermeyer continues], completely stymied the translator responsible for *99 Limericks,* a recent collection published by a firm in Munich, with the limericks published in English plus German translations and learned commentaries in Germanic prose.

Aubrey Beardsley

Thereupon he resorted to *two* translations. In one the word "spring" was given as *Früjahr* (the season), in the other it became *Quelle* (a flow of water), while "fall" was rendered as both *Herbst* (the season) and *Wasserfall* (waterfall).

As we have indicated, the best limericks should satisfy us by their unexpected solutions to rhyming problems, and they should delight us with a surprise ending. If the thought can be anticipated before the climax is reached, if the punch comes too early, the limerick is weakened. The real trick is a neat combination of metrical perfection, verbal felicity and a quick turn of wit. Without these, even the bawdiest limerick becomes stale and unprofitable.

André Domin

III *Origins:*

"There was a sick man of Tobago . . ."

The origins of the limericks are shrouded in mystery.

F. A. Wright, in a book titled *Greek Social Life,* suggests that the limerick goes back to Aristophanes (448?-?380 B.C.), the greatest of the Greek comic poets. In *The Wasps,* Wright writes, there is a scene near the end in which the characters of the play are taking part in a symposium. (Our dictionary defines symposium as "a drinking together; a convivial feast or banquet.") One of the characters at this drinking together, then, describes a chariot accident on the streets of Athens which Mr. Wright translates into modern American times and terms as:

> An amateur, driving too fast,
> From his car to the roadway was cast,
>   And a friend kindly said,
>   As he banged his head,
> "Mr. Cobbler, stick to your last."[1]

". . . I do not insist"—it is Gershon Legman speaking—"that 'Sumer is i-cumen in' (about 1300),

---

1. Mr. Wright adds that although the tipple of these roistering Athenians was only wine "copiously diluted with water," the company rarely dispersed until day-break.

the oldest popular song in the English language, is
in limerick form, but a rather good case can be
made for its stanzaic portion at least, and the pos-
sibility ought not to be overlooked."

"Sumer is i-cumen in" includes, in the stanzaic
portion:

> Ewè bleateth after lamb,
> Low'th after calvè coo;
>   Bullock starteth,
>   Buckè farteth—
> Merry sing cuckoo!

Legman goes on to cite *The Making of Verse*
(1934) by Robert Swann and Frank Sidgwick, who
discovered another early animal limerick in the
British Museum's Harleian Manuscript 7322, dating from the 14th century:

> The lion is wonderliche strong,
> & ful of wiles of wo;
>   & whether he pleye
>   other take his preye
> He can not do but slo.[2]

2. Read "slay."

Some two centuries seem then to have passed before the limerick put in a reappearance in "the mad-songs of the half-naked wandering beggars, turned out to mump their livelihood after 1536, at the dissolution of the religious almonries under Henry VIII" (Legman).

In Legman's authoritative opinion, the greatest of these songs is "Mad Tom," or "Tom o' Bedlam," first recorded in Giles Earle's manuscript music book about 1615, although probably decades older by then. The song is in the limerick form throughout:

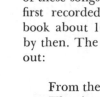

> From the hagg & hungry Goblin,
> That into raggs would rend yee,
>   & the spirit that stands
>   by the naked man,
> In the booke of moones defend yee . . .

Some students of the form hold that Shakespeare wrote a limerick in *Othello,* which is to be dated 1604. In Act II, Scene 3, Lines 68-72, Iago, to gain his private ends, is plying Cassio with liquor. The tough old top-sergeant sings a song which, he de-

clares, he picked up in England, where "they are
most potent in potting":

> And let the canikin clink, clink;
> And let the canakin clink.
>   A soldier's a man;
>   O man's life's but a span;
> Why then let a soldier drink.

Nor is this an isolated instance: Edgar, disguised
as "poor Tom" in *King Lear* chants a spell to the
rhythm of "Tom o'Bedlam";—there is also Ste-
phano's song in *The Tempest*—"For she had a
tongue with a tang"—and Ophelia's touching mad-
song in *Hamlet*—"His beard was white as snow."
    Ben Jonson, too, explored the form in his
Masque of the Gypsies Metamorphos'd—"The faery
became uppon you"—and so did Robert Herrick:

> Her Eyes the Glow-worme lend thee,
> The Shooting-Starres attend thee;
>   And the elves alsó
>   Whose little eyes glow
> Like the sparke of fire, befriend thee . . .

Aubrey Beardsley

A limerick which bears many of the trademarks of the form as we know it today—anapestic rhythm and proper names setting the rhymes, to mention only two—is "Mondayes Work" from the *Roxburghe Ballads*, published in broadside form by 1640, and it begins:

> Good morrow, neighbour Gamble,
> Come let you and I goe ramble:
>   Last night I was shot
>   Through the braines with a pot
> And now my stomach doth wamble . . .

According to Legman, the earliest *geographical* limerick (by far the largest class, as well as one of the oldest) yet discovered seems to have appeared in *The Midwife, or Old Woman's Magazine*, about 1750. It was reprinted in *The Nonpareil* in 1757 and four years later (1761) in *The New Boghouse Miscellany*. It is titled "On Jollity," and it begins:

There was a jovial butcher,
Who liv'd at Northern-fall-gate,
    He kept a stall
    At Leadenhall
And got drunk at the Boy at Aldgate . . .

Finally, in this brief case for England as the birthplace of the limerick, let us note that Carolyn Wells wrote—on what authority she did not say—that the limerick about the Young Man of St. Kitts was very popular "in 1834." It goes:

There was a young man of St. Kitts,
Who was very much troubled with fits;
    The eclipse of the moon
    Threw him into a swoon;
When he tumbled and broke into bits.

To turn now to another point of view, let us consider Ireland by way of France as the originating locale of the limerick—a theory whose greatest exponent was the late collector, compiler and creator of limericks, (Herbert) Langford Reed. According to Reed, the Typhoid Marys of the limer-

Aubrey Beardsley

ick were the returned veterans of the Irish Brigade —an outfit which had been serving with the French Army for a hundred years or so after 1691, when Patrick Sarsfield, after surrendering Limerick, Ireland, to King William's men, took a lot of the stout fellows who had been fighting for King James over the Channel to fight for Louis XIV.

This of course would mean that the limerick must have been a long-established form of verse in France, and, to place it there, Reed cited from a footnote in Chapter 47 of Boswell's *Life of Johnson* an epigram lifted from the *Ménagiana* (1715) about a young lady who went to a masquerade ball dressed as a Jesuit. (The masquerade ball is to this day one of the most popular settings for the incidents described in limericks.) The gist of the limerick is that the lady who is parading as an arch conservative is really a liberal and is therefore improperly dressed:

> On s'étonne ici que Caliste
> Ait pris l'habit de Moliniste
>   Puisque cette jeune beauté
>   Ote à chacun sa liberté
> N'est ce pas une Janseniste?

In this same connection, Reed quoted a French version of "Hickory, Dickory, Dock":

Digerie, digerie, doge.
La souris ascend l'horloge.
L'horloge frappe
La souris s'échappe,
Digerie, digerie, doge.

Reed then made the important point that the limerick was originally *sung,* not recited: each member of the group would come forward in turn and chant a limerick, which was followed by a chorus (or challenge) sung by the entire audience, usually to the tune of "The Spanish Nobilio," better known in America as "The Gay Caballero":

That was a very nice song,
Sing us another one—
Just like the other one—
Sing us another one, do!

(Your editor well recalls a vaudeville act, very popular on the Keith-Orpheum circuit *circa* 1923, which presented as one of its "production num-

André Domin

André Domin

bers" just such an entertainment, with the identical chorus given above.)

In America, the chorus is more recently to the tune of "Cielito lindo":

> Aye, yi, yi-yi!!—
> In China they never eat chili;
> So here's to the next verse,
> Much worse than the last verse,
> And waltz me around again, Willie!

According to Legman, the British connecting chorus goes:

> Now hear, all ye dukes and ye duchesses,
>   Take heed of my warning, I say,
> Be sure that you owns all you touches-es,
>   Or I'll land you in Botany Bay!

The point here, according to Reed, is that the veterans of the Irish Brigade, after their return to Limerick, that lively town on the banks of the Shannon, just west of Tipperary, sang their limericks at convivial gatherings impromptu, with a chorus which always went:

Won't you come up, come up,
Won't you come up, I say,
Won't you come up, come all the way up,
Come all the way up to Limerick?

Hence, Reed wrote, the name "limerick" for this confection. So convinced was he that Limerick was the true home of the limerick that he saluted the town in a verse (a limerick, naturally):

All hail to the town of Limerick
Which provides a cognomen, generic,
    For a species of verse
    Which, for better or worse,
Is supported by layman and cleric.[3]

The word "limerick" officially entered the English language, according to the *Oxford English Dictionary*, in 1898, in which year a Mr. J. H. Murray, in response to a question voiced in *Notes & Queries*, defined the limerick as an "indecent nonsense verse." Legman, on the other hand, pinpoints the coinage of the name "as at some time between 1882 and 1898, possibly in the columns of the sporting newspaper, *The Pink 'Un* (a sort of British *Police*

3. It's been said that the only English word for which there is no rhyme is the word "oblige." All hail to Reed, nonetheless, for making no effort to avoid finding a rhyme for "limerick."

Hail, too, to the anonymous author of:

There was a young farmer of Limerick
Who started one day to trim a rick.
    The Fates gave a frown,
    The rick tumbled down,
And killed him—I don't know a grimmer trick.

And to Elmo Calkins, who wrote:

Pray search this wide land with a glimmer stick
For there must be some lad at his primer quick,
    Who when pressed can supply
    A lot better than I
An acceptable rhyme scheme for "limerick."

Gazette; both being imitations of earlier French *risqué* journals on colored pulp, such as *Le Piron*) . . ."

Carolyn Wells damned the Limerick = limerick theory as "a mere fancy, founded in no truth whatever," and Monsignor Knox and many other authorities have also refused to accept this explanation. Their grounds—and they are good ones—are that there is nothing in the chorus reputedly sung in Limerick that fits the meter or the pattern of the limerick—it might well have been a challenge to sing a bawdier *ballad.*

Nevertheless, says Morris Bishop, whose opinion in this field is always to be respected:

. . . a few hours in the library have revealed to me some substantiation. In Kathleen Hoagland's *1000 Years of Irish Poetry* I have found some perfect limericks translated from the Irish. Here is one stanza, to the air of "The Growling Old Woman," by John O'Tuomy (1706-77), who was an innkeeper in Limerick:

I sell the best brandy and sherry
To make good customers merry;

But at times their finances
Run short, as it chances,
And then I feel very sad, very.

Edward Lysaght, Esq., "Pleasant Ned Lysaght," was a barrister-at-law on the Munster
Circuit about 1800. (His daughter married the
Lord Bishop of Limerick.) His *Poems,* published in 1811, include a serious celebration of
Ireland in limerick form and also a series of
limericks in Irish.

These indications, though tenuous, hint that
the limerick form was actually existent in the
city of Limerick . . . .

In any case, the first existing book of limericks
(not of course called limericks in the book) was
published in London by John Harris in 1821. It is
titled *The History of Sixteen Wonderful Old
Women,* and all sixteen of the old women are not
only wonderful; they are also exemplary. Here is
one of them:

André Domin

Aubrey Beardsley

There was an old woman of Leeds
Who spent all her life in good deeds;
    She worked for the poor
     Till her fingers were sore,
This pious old woman of Leeds.

The History of Sixteen Wonderful Old Women was followed the next year (1822) by *Anecdotes and Adventures of Fifteen Gentlemen* (written by R. S. Sharpe?, with drawings by Robert Cruikshank?), published by John Marshall of London. As we shall see in our next chapter, one of these fifteen gentlemen was to have a profound effect on the future of the limerick. He was the Sick Man of Tobago, mentioned by Dickens in the second chapter of *Our Mutual Friend,* and his story goes:

There was a sick man of Tobago,
Who liv'd long on rice-gruel and sago;
    But at last, to his bliss,
     The physician said this—
"To a roast leg of mutton you may go."

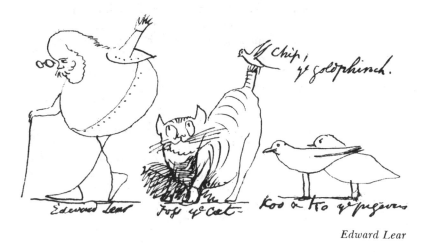

Edward Lear

IV *The Founding Father:*

"There once was an artist named Lear . . ."

EDWARD LEAR, "The Poet Laureate of the Limerick," was born in Highgate on May 12, 1812, the youngest of a family of twenty-one children. He died on January 29, 1888, at San Remo on the Italian Riviera, where he had lived for the last eighteen of his long (almost 76) years of life.

At the early age of fifteen, Lear was earning his living as a commercial artist, mostly by illustrating the writings of others.[1] Some paintings of birds Lear had made for the ornithologist John Gould attracted the attention of Edward Stanley, the thirteenth Earl of Derby, who wanted an artist to make the pictures for a book he was thinking of writing about the menagerie which was a showplace of the Earl's estate at Knowsley near Liverpool.

Edward Lear was to work for no less than four successive Earls of Derby. Far more important, he was to spend much of his leisure time amusing the grandchildren, nephews and nieces of the thirteenth Earl to whom his first *Book of Nonsense* (1846) is dedicated.

Lear never pretended to have invented the rhyme scheme we now call the limerick, nor did

---

1. At one time Lear was drawing master to Queen Victoria. In limerick form, H. I. Brock has described what happened:

> There once was an artist named Lear
> Who wrote verses to make children cheer.
>   Though they never made sense,
>   Their success was immense,
> And the Queen thought that Lear was a dear.

he ever use the word "limerick." To the contrary, he made it quite clear that his use of the form was inspired by reading "There was a sick man of Tobago." He himself wrote that he found it "a form of verse lending itself to limitless varieties for rhymes and pictures; and thenceforth the great part of the original drawings and verses for the first *Book of Nonsense* were struck off."[2]

Lear saw three additional volumes published during his own lifetime: *Nonsense Songs, Stories, Botany and Alphabets* (1871); *More Nonsense, Pictures, Rhymes, Botany, Etc.* (1872); and *Laughable Lyrics, A Fourth Book of Nonsense Poems, Songs, Botany, Music, Etc.* (1877). A fifth of his books, *Nonsense Songs and Stories,* was not published until 1895.

Lear's limericks—he wrote, in all, 212 of them—are to be found only in the books of 1846 and 1872, but all five volumes will vastly reward the reader of nonsense verse. For here are some of the classics of the *genre:* "The Owl and the Pussy-Cat," "The Jumblies," "Calico Pie," "The Dong with the Luminous Nose," "The Pobble Who Has No Toes," "The Pelican Chorus," "Mr. and Mrs. Discobbolos," "The Akand of Swat" and "Incidents in the

Edward Lear

2. Holbrook Jackson, one of Lear's biographers (see his Introduction to *The Complete Nonsense of Edward Lear*), has said that "It is easier to find a First Folio Shakespeare than a first edition of *A Book of Nonsense;* even the British Museum Library has to content itself with a copy of the third edition (1861)."

Edward Lear

3. This was true: Lear was a grumbler. No doubt he had good reason to be: he was a chronic epileptic, who lived much of his life in fear.

Life of My Uncle Arly." Here, too, is Edward Lear's own self-portrait:

> How pleasant to know Mr. Lear,
>   Who has written such volumes of stuff!
> Some think him ill-tempered and queer,[3]
>   But a few think him pleasant enough.
>
> His mind is concrete and fastidious,
>   His nose is remarkably big;
> His visage is more or less hideous,
>   His beard it resembles a wig.
>
> He has ears, and two eyes, and ten fingers,
>   Leastways if you reckon two thumbs;
> Long ago he was one of the singers,
>   But now he is one of the dumbs.
>
> He sits in a beautiful parlour,
>   With hundreds of books on the wall;
> He drinks a great deal of Marsala,
>   But he never gets tipsy at all.

He has many friends, laymen and clerical;
    Old Foss is the name of his cat;[4]
His body is perfectly spherical,
    He weareth a runcible hat.

When he walks in a waterproof white,
    The children run after him so!
Calling out, "He's come out in his night-
    Gown, that crazy old Englishman, oh!"

He weeps by the side of the ocean,
    He weeps on the top of the hill;
He purchases pancakes and lotion,
    And chocolate shrimps from the mill.

He reads but he cannot speak Spanish,
    He cannot abide ginger beer;
Ere the days of his pilgrimage vanish,
    How pleasant to know Mr. Lear!

Louis Untermeyer has written, quite correctly, that Lear, despite the endless possibilities he saw in the limerick,

Edward Lear

4. Lear's last book contains "The Heraldic Blazon of Foss the Cat." "Foss," says Holbrook Jackson, "lived to the advanced age of seventeen years. He received honourable burial with a suitably inscribed headstone in the garden of Lear's villa at San Remo."

scarcely took advantage of them. Part of the charm of the limerick is the surprise, the sudden swoop and unexpected twist of the last line. With few exceptions, Lear ignored the whiplash ending which makes the modern limerick so effective. He rarely introduced a new rhyme at the conclusion; practically all his last lines are repetitions or slight variations of the first line.

Nonetheless, Lear's limericks set the pattern for many years to come—a fact that dismayed him. As Langford Reed put it:

> A goddess capricious is Fame.
> You may strive to make noted your name.
>   But she either neglects you
>   Or coolly selects you
> For laurels distinct from your aim!

Here, now, are a few of the limericks by Lear—"Learics," if you prefer—which over the years have proved themselves most popular with collectors. First, from *A Book of Nonsense:*

Edward Lear

There was an Old Man with a beard,
Who said, "It is just as I feared—
    Two Owls and a Hen,
    Four Larks and a Wren,
Have all built their nests in my beard!"

There was a Young Lady of Ryde,
Whose shoe-strings were seldom untied;
    She purchased some clogs,
    And some small spotty dogs,
And frequently walked about Ryde.[5]

There was an Old Man who supposed
That the street door was partially closed;
    But some very large rats
    Ate his coats and his hats,
While that futile old gentleman dozed.

There was a Young Lady from Norway
Who casually sat in a doorway;
    When the door squeezed her flat,
    She exclaimed, "What of that?"
This courageous Young Lady of Norway.

[5]. This limerick by Lear undoubtedly inspired the anonymous authors of two mildly less proper versions:

There was a fat lady of Clyde
Whose shoelaces once came untied;
    She feared that to bend
    Would display her rear end,
So she cried and she cried and she cried.

There was a fat lady of Bryde
Whose shoelaces once came untied;
    She didn't dare stoop
    For fear she would poop,
So she cried and she cried and she cried.

There was an Old Man of Cape Horn,
Who wished he had never been born;
  So he sat on a chair,
  Till he died of despair,
That dolorous Man of Cape Horn.

There was an Old Man of Dundee,
Who frequented the top of a tree;
  When disturbed by the crows,
  He abruptly arose,
And exclaimed, "I'll return to Dundee!"

There was an Old Man who said, "Hush!
I perceive a young bird in this bush!"
  When they said, "Is it small?"
  He replied, "Not at all!
It is four times as big as the bush!"

There was an Old Man with a beard,
Who sat on a horse when he reared;
  But they said, "Never mind!
  You will fall off behind,
You propitious Old Man with a beard!"[6]

Edward Lear

6. The bearded Lear was obviously immoderately fond of old men with beards.

And these are from *More Nonsense, Pictures, Rhymes, Botany, Etc.*:

> There was an old person of Ware
> Who rode on the back of a bear:
>   When they asked—"Does it trot?"
>   He said, "Certainly not!
> He's a Moppsikon Floppsikon bear!"[7]

> There was a young lady of Greenwich,
> Whose garments were border'd with spinach;
>   But a large Spotty Calf
>   Bit her shawl quite in half,
> Which alarmed that young lady of Greenwich.

And here, for our last limerick by the founding father, is the famous Old Man of Thermopylae:

Edward Lear

7. After Lewis Carroll, Lear was almost certainly the greatest coiner of nonsense words in the English language. He gave us "scroobius," "meloobius," "ombliferous," "borascible," "slobaciously," "himmeltanious," "flumpetty," "mumbian," and many others.

There was an old man of Thermopylae,
Who never did anything properly;
  But they said, "If you choose
  To boil eggs in your shoes,
You shall never remain in Thermopylae."

Ave atque vale, Edward Lear!

Edward Lear

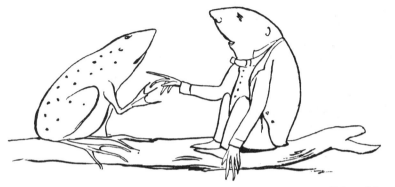

V *The Limerick, Laundered, in the Nineteenth Century:*

"I shall, with cultured taste . . ."

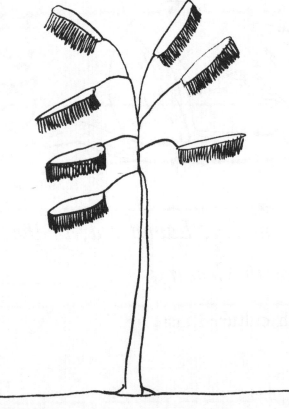

Edward Lear

TRUTH TO TELL, the 1846 edition of Edward Lear's *A Book of Nonsense* created no great stir. But the reprint edition of almost twenty years later—1863 —inspired *Punch* to open its columns to the limerick of propriety.

The first number of *Punch* was dated July 17, 1841, but it was not until December, 1845, that the first limerick appeared in its pages. It concerns Henry Lord Brougham and Vaux, Lord Chancellor of England, who played a leading part in carrying through the Reform Bill of 1832:

> There was an old broom of St. Stephen's,
> That set all at sixes and sevens;
>   And to sweep from the room
>   The convictions of Brougham,
> Was the work of this Broom of St. Stephen's.

After this inauspicious start, *Punch* did little with the form until 1863. Then, with the appearance of the reprint edition of *A Book of Nonsense,* it announced that it would immortalize all the place names in England with a "rhyme." This series lasted only two months, however, and ran to a mere thirty-three limericks.

Punch then virtually dropped the form till March, 1902, when the verse form was restored to favor with the first of a new series of "Literary Limericks."

From this time on, *Punch* was to specialize in what Clifton Fadiman was later to call "The Limerick of Co-ordinated Orthography"—the type of limerick which sees humorous possibilities in abbreviations and unorthodox spellings. Here, from *Punch,* are three examples:

There was a young chappie named Cholmon-
       deley,
Who always at dinner sat dolmondesley;
    His fair partner said,
    As he crumbled his bread,
"Dear me! you behave very rolmondeley!"

Said a man to his spouse in East Sydenham,
"My best trousers! Now where have you hyden-
       ham?
    It is perfectly true
    They were not very new
But I foolishly left half a quidenham."

Edward Lear

A charming young lady named Geoghegan
Whose Christian names are less peophegan
    Will be Mrs. Knollys
    Very soon at All Ksollys;
But the date is at present a veogheg'un.

English wits—particularly Oxford and Cambridge wits, both students and dons—were quick to take up the form. At Cambridge, for example, in 1872, appeared a rare magazine called *Light Green,* two issues of which were published. For it, "a short-lived genius" named A. C. Hilton wrote:

There was a young gourmand of Johns
Who'd a notion of dining on swans.
    To the Backs he took big nets
    To capture the cygnets
But was told they were kept for the dons.

Even more important to the development of the limerick were the contributions by clergymen. William Ralph Inge, Dean of St. Paul's Cathedral from 1911 to 1934, whose pessimism earned him the title of "the gloomy dean," was only one of many men of the cloth who found amusement in the form:

His most famous limerick is about the Old Man of
Khartoum, which some—remembering a comment
of Sir Richard Burton's in the tenth volume of his
"translation" of *A Thousand Nights and a Night
(The Arabian Nights Entertainment)*— have found
slightly suggestive:

> There was an old man of Khartoum
> Who kept two tame sheep in his room,
>   To remind him, he said,
>   Of two friends who were dead;
> But he could not remember of whom.

In America, the minor writer Charles Godfrey
Leland, who was later (1877) to write a book called
Johnnykin and the Goblins, an unabashed imitation of Lewis Carroll's *Alice in Wonderland,* issued
in 1863 *Ye Book of Copperheads,* published by
Leypoldt of Philadelphia, a volume of satirical
limericks directed against Lincoln and the "copperheads"—those Northerners sympathetic to the
Southern cause during the Civil War.

In the same year there appeared a set of "Nursery Rhymes for the Army" in a book called *Spirit
of the Times*—twenty-three limericks signed L. L. D.,

Edward Lear

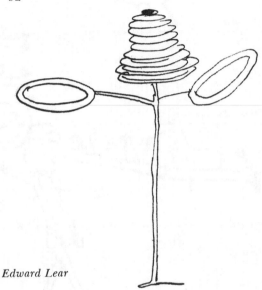

Edward Lear

1. Holmes, a physician as well as a poet and a lecturer, is said to have done his medical career little good by once remarking that he was grateful for small fevers.

"initials that may possibly represent Leland's name with the vowels omitted," surmises Gershon Legman.

Almost immediately after (March, 1864), a much more widely circulated imitation appeared, this time acknowledging Lear's inspiration in the title, *The New Book of Nonsense,* and was followed in June, 1864, by *Ye Book of Bubbles* and *Inklings for Thinklings.* All three of these volumes were published in Philadelphia to aid the Sanitary Commission of the Great Central Fair which was held to benefit sufferers from the Civil War.

By the end of the nineteenth century, certainly, the limerick had firmly established itself in both Britain and America, and hardly a literary figure of the times had failed to try his hand at it.

That "Autocrat of the Breakfast Table," Oliver Wendell Holmes, Sr. (1809-94), a man noted for his punning,[1] is credited with a limerick that is still among the most quoted (Bennett Cerf has included it in his collection, *Out on a Limerick,* as one of the all-time "Big Ten"):

The Reverend Henry Ward Beecher
Called a hen a most elegant creature,
    The hen, pleased with that,
      Laid an egg in his hat—
And thus did the hen reward Beecher.

The Reverend Charles Lutwidge Dodgson, better known as "Lewis Carroll" (1832-98), the only man in the field of nonsense verse who might be called superior to Lear, must have found the limerick form to his liking, too, for he wrote:

There was a young man of Oporta,
Who daily got shorter and shorter.
    The reason, he said,
      Was the hod on his head,
Which was filled with the heaviest mortar.

Thanks to the Mark Twain Society, there are any number of limericks about Samuel Langhorne Clemens (1835-1910),[2] but the only limerick Twain seems to have written is:

2. In the 1940's, the Society instituted a nationwide contest for the best limerick on its patron saint. More than three thousand candidates were submitted. The prize was awarded to Mrs. W. S. Burgess of Fullerton, Nebraska, for:

Mark Twain was a mop-headed male,
Whose narratives sparkled like ale;
    And this Prince of the Grin
    Who once fathered Huck Finn
Can still hold the world by the tale!

A man hired by John Smith and Co.
Loudly declared he would tho.
   Man that he saw
   Dumping dirt near his store.
The drivers, therefore, didn't do.

Twain's contemporary, the short-story writer Thomas Bailey Aldrich (1836-1907) gave us:

There was a young woman of Aenos
Who came to our party as Venus.
   We told her how rude
   'Twas to come there quite nude,
And we brought her a leaf from the green-h'us.

Back in England, Sir William Schwenck Gilbert (1836-1911), perhaps the most nimble rhymer of his age, made a close approach to the limerick in his early *Bab Ballads*. "The Story of Prince Agib," for example, goes in part:

Of Agib, who amid Tartaric scenes,
Wrote a lot of ballet music in his teens:
   His gentle spirit rolls

Edward Lear

In the melody of souls—
Which is pretty, but I don't know what it means.

Gilbert came even closer to composing a limerick in *The Yeoman of the Guard*—"A man who would woo a fair maid / Should 'prentice himself to the trade . . ."—and closer still in the duet sung by Bunthorne and Grosvenor in Act II of *Patience*. The last five lines of Bunthorne's first stanza read:

I shall, with cultured taste,
Distinguish gems from paste,
   And "High diddle diddle"
   Will rank as an idyll
If I pronounce it chaste!

Best of all is this song from *The Sorcerer:*

Oh, my name is John Wellington Wells,
I'm a dealer in magic and spells,
   In blessings and curses,
   And ever-filled purses,
In prophecies, witches, and knells.

If you want a proud foe to "make tracks"—
If you'd melt a rich uncle in wax—
    You've but to look in
    On our resident Djinn,
Number seventy, Simmery Axe . . .

This last would seem to have influenced the oc-
cultist and self-styled "worst man in the world,"
Aleister Crowley, to write, in addition to seventeen
obscene limericks, the parody:

My name it is Aleister Crowley,
I'm a master of Magick unholy,
    Of philtres and pentacles,
    Covens, conventicles;
Of basil, nepenthe, and moly.

And Gilbert is said to have written an authentic
limerick in the rather feeble:

There was a Professor named Chesterton,
Who went for a walk with his best shirt on.
    Being hungry he ate it,
    But lived to regret it,
And ruined his life for his digesterton.

Still, there is some evidence that the always irascible Gilbert had little patience with the limerick as practiced by Lear. Lear had written, in *A Book of Nonsense:*

> There was an old man in a tree,
> Who was horribly bored by a bee.
>> When they said, "Does it buzz?"
>> He replied, "Yes, it does!
> It's a regular brute of a bee."

To this Gilbert retorted:

> There was an old man of St. Bees,
> Who was stung in the arm by a Wasp.
>> When asked, "Does it hurt?"
>> He replied, "No, it doesn't;
> I'm *so* glad that it wasn't a Hornet."

This limerick has also been credited to George Bernard Shaw (1856-1950). Shaw, a confirmed limerick lover, bemoaned the fact that so many of his favorite limericks were, in his day, "unfit for publication." "They must be left," he wrote, "for oral tradition, but it may be that, in the course of time,

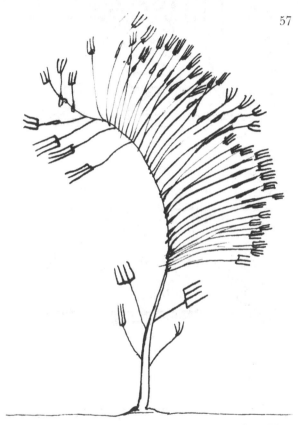

Edward Lear

sufficient limericks which shall be decent as well as witty or ingenious may accumulate."

While no limerick *by* Shaw seems to have come down to us, there are any number *about* him, including this one by Coulson Kernahan:

> A poodle was charged by the law
> With resembling Hall Caine. With his paw
>   Pressed close to his forehead,
>   He sobbed, "Yes, it's horrid,
> But at least I'm not George Bernard Shaw!"

And this one by Patrick Braybrooke, F.R.S.L.:

> Than Shakespeare I'm greater by far.
> I am always produced by a star.
>   My plots he can find 'em—
>   For I am behind 'em.
> It's "in front" they don't know what they are!

And this one from *Punch* (1918):

> There was a young man of Moose Jaw
> Who wanted to meet Bernard Shaw;

Edward Lear

When they questioned him, "Why?"
He made no reply,
But sharpened an ax and a saw.

Robert Louis Stevenson (1850-94) is known to have written at least one limerick, which perhaps helped to take the "place-name" variety of the form out of the British Isles and extend its range to other parts of the world. It goes:

There was an old man of the Cape
Who made himself garments of crepe.
When asked, "Do they tear?"
He replied, "Here and there;
But they're perfectly splendid for shape."[3]

Eugene Field (1850-95) is best remembered today (in public) as the creator of the Rock-a-By Lady from Hushaby Land and the Shut-Eye Train for Shut-Eye Town, but he is perhaps more warmly remembered (in private) as the creator of such erotica as "Only a Boy," "Socratic Love," and "The Fair Limousin'"—the latter one of the well-known

3. Attributed to Mrs. Evans Nepean in her book, *The Day of Small Things*, by Langford Reed in his *Complete Limerick Book*. And, compare here the later limerick:

A thrifty young fellow of Shoreham
Made brown paper trousers and woreham;
He looked nice and neat
Till he bent in the street
To pick up a pin; then he toreham.

sources of synonyms for sexual intercourse. But Field, who earned a part of his living for many years as a theatrical critic, also wrote nursery-clean limericks, including:

'Tis strange how the newspapers honor
A creature that's called prima donna.
 They say not a thing
 Of how she can sing
But write reams of the clothes she has on her.

Another of Field's limericks—

Now what in the world shall we dioux
With the bloody and murderous Sioux,
 Who some time ago
 Took an arrow and bow
And raised such a hellabelioux?

inspired any number of imitations, one of them the limerick sequence, "Prevalent Poetry" (included in Carolyn Wells' *A Whimsey Anthology*):

A wandering tribe, called the Siouxs,
Wear moccasins, having no shiouxs,

They are made of buckskin,
With the fleshy side in,
Embroidered with beads of bright hyiouxs.

When out on the warpath, the Siouxs
March single file—never by tiouxs—
    And by "blazing" the trees
    Can return at their ease,
And their way through the forests ne'er liouxs.

All new-fashioned boats he exchiouxs,
And uses the birch-bark caniouxs;
    These are handy and light,
    And, inverted at night,
Give shelter from storms and from dyiouxs.

The principal food of the Siouxs
Is Indian maize, which they briouxs
    And hominy make,
    Or mix in a cake,
And eat it with forks, as they chiouxs.

It must not be thought, however, that the creation of limericks in the nineteenth century was re-
stricted to writing men alone. Take, for example,

Aubrey Beardsley

André Domin

this limerick by the American artist resident in London from 1863 on, James Abbott McNeill Whistler (1834-1903):

> There is a creator named God
> Whose doings are sometimes quite odd.
>   He made a painter named Val,
>   And I say—and I shall—
> That he does no great credit to God.

Who "Val" was, we do not know, but we do know that Whistler himself—a man who had a genius for saying and doing the wrong things—was the victim of this limerick by his fellow artist (and poet) Dante Gabriel Rossetti (1828-82), who also created many other limericks, proper and bawdy:

> There is a young artist named Whistler
> Who in every respect is a bristler;
>   A tube of white lead
>   Or a punch in the head
> Come equally handy to Whistler.

André Domin

VI *The Limerick, Laundered, in the Twentieth Century:*

"There was a young lady of Ryde . . ."

Aubrey Beardsley

DURING THE LATTER HALF of 1907 and the first half of 1908 the fad of the limerick was given tremendous impetus by contests conducted by newspapers and other periodicals, particularly *London Opinion,* and by manufacturers to promote their products.

Usually, the first four lines of a limerick were given, and the public was invited to write the tag line.

In one such contest, the incomplete limerick ran as follows:

> There was a young lady of Ryde,
> Whose locks were consid'rably dyed.
>> The hue of her hair
>> Made everyone stare . . .

Perhaps the best of the ten winners, each of whom received about £50 (then worth about $250), submitted this:

> "She's piebald, she'll die bald!" they cried.

In the case of the newspaper contests, it was customary to ask each competitor to forward as an entrance fee a postal order for sixpence. "The public, in the last six months of the year [1907] would have bought, in the ordinary way, between 700,000 and 800,000 six-penny postal orders," said a Mr. Buxton during a speech he made before the House of Commons on July 17, 1908. "They . . . actually bought no less than 11,400,000—fourteen times as much!"

The craze soon assumed the proportions of a business, with its own "professors" who, for a fee, were prepared to supply last lines "practically certain" to win. (Much the same sort of thing happened during the celebrated Old Gold Cigarette Puzzle Contest of 1937 and later contests sponsored principally by U. S. newspapers.)

And the prizes in many of the competitions were well worth winning. Traylee Cigarettes, for example, offered *£3 a week for life.* (Of course, each entrant had to submit with his last line a coupon proving that he had purchased a half-crown's worth of the cigarettes.)

The incomplete limerick in this contest ran:

> That the Traylee's the best cigarette,
> Is a "tip" that we cannot forget.

And in buying, I'll mention
There's a three pound a week pension . . .

The winner, whose name was announced in the
Westminster Gazette of October 23, 1907, was a Mr.
R. Rhodes of Romilly Road, Cardiff, Wales, who
submitted:

Two good "lines"—one you give, one you get.

So successful was this contest that Mr. Samuda,
the manufacturer of Traylee Cigarettes, promptly
launched a second contest. The first prize in this
competition was three-fold: a freehold house, a
horse and trap, and £2 a week for life. The house
was highly desirable, judging by the description
given in the advertisement that announced the contest:

A pretty, well-kept country villa standing in
its own grounds, decorated and furnished
throughout by Waring & Gillow, and containing kitchen, drawing-room, dining-room and
bedrooms, with everything in it conducive to

home comfort. Table linen, crockery, household utensils, bed-linen, draperies—all are included. Every modern improvement, including bathroom (h. and c.), electric light, etc.

Years later, in America, in 1930, a long series of limerick contests in *Liberty* magazine inspired Kenneth R. Close to compose a handbook called *How to Write Prize-Winning Limericks* (Coral Gables, Florida: University of Miami).

While limerick contests are no longer as fashionable as they once were, one was very successfully conducted as recently as 1965 among creative men and women in advertising agencies for the magazine *Business Week* by its Promotion Director, Mr. Martin Kaiden. This contest differed from the older variety in that it required those who entered it to write *the first four lines* of a limerick ending: "It isn't how many . . . it's *who*." There was a second prize of $500, a third prize of $250, twelve honorable mentions (portable typewriters) and the grand prize—a round trip for two to Limerick, Ireland:

Aubrey Beardsley

Leave New York aboard Irish International Airlines and land at Shannon Airport in time for a traditional Irish Coffee greeting and a visit to the duty-free shops. Feast like a lord in medieval splendor at the 15th century Bunratty Castle. Sleep in the refurbished elegance of historic Dromoland Castle. Tour the famous Clare coast with its championship golf courses and be the luncheon guest of honor of the Mayor of Limerick. Wend your way to Killarney and Cork and have a try at the Blarney Stone. Meet the Lord Mayor of Dublin and spend an evening at the Abbey Theatre. In short, have a broth of a good time for two weeks—on *Business Week*. And take $500 in spending money from us, too.

Of course, if you'd rather, you may substitute the whole adventure for $2,500 in emerald-green bills . . .

There were 1,443 entrants who submitted "over 4,200 darlin' limericks." First prize was won by

Alexander I. Ross, Vice President of Al Lefton
Company, Inc., New York City, for:

> If it's management men you pursue
> Don't hunt every beast in the zoo—
>   Just look for the signs
>   That say: "Tigers and Lions."
> It isn't how many . . . it's *who*.

While the limerick, in our own century, in both
Britain and America, seems to have had an extraordinary appeal for anyone capable of creating
witty and ingenious verse, it was the professional
writers who continued to turn out the more lasting
examples.

Padraic Colum, writing in *Esquire* (March, 1936)
cites this limerick by the Irish novelist George
Moore (1852-1933):

> My neighbors, the dirty Miss Drews,
> Stand on their doorstep and muse,
>   And tie up their tresses
>   While the dogs make their messes,
> And I am wiping my shoes.

André Domin

André Domin

Oliver Herford (1863-1935), author and illustrator and the Number One wit of The Players Club for many years, wrote at least three highly memorable limericks:

A damsel, seductive and handsome,
Got wedged in a sleeping-room transom.
    When she offered much gold
    For release, she was told
That the view was worth more than the ransom.

There once were some learned M. D.'s
Who captured some germs of disease
    And infected a train,
    Which, without causing pain,
Allowed hundreds to catch it with ease.

There was a young lady of Twickenham
Whose shoes were too tight to walk quick in 'em.
    She came back from a walk
    Looking whiter than chalk
And took 'em both off and was sick in 'em.

As President of The Players, Herford imposed a
rule on members while within the club—"Not a
word that's profane or obscene," a canon that H. I.
Brock took to heart in compiling his *Little Book of
Limericks*. Wrote Brock in his envoi to that book:

> In this book every line has been clean;
> Not a word that's profane or obscene,
>   Or spelled in four letters
>   That might pain our betters,
> Or snafu—if you know what we mean.[1]

Rudyard Kipling (1865-1936) referred to the limerick in his *Stalky* ("Make up a good Limerick, and
let the fags sing it"), and himself authored a limerick:

> There once was a boy of Quebec
> Who was buried in snow to his neck.
>   When asked, "Are you frizz?"
>   He replied, "Yes, I is,
> But we don't call this cold in Quebec."

1. "Snafu"—World War II word meaning "Situation
normal: all fouled [euphemism] up."

André Domin

Gelett Burgess (1866-1951), creator of "The Goops" and the man who added such words as "blurb" and "bromide" to the English language, is perhaps best remembered today for "The Purple Cow" and its sequel:

> I never saw a Purple Cow,
>   I never hope to see one;
> But I can tell you, anyhow,
>   I'd rather see than be one.

> Ah, yes, I wrote the "Purple Cow"—
>   I'm sorry, now, I wrote it!
> But I can tell you, anyhow,
>   I'll kill you if you quote it.

But Burgess was also a celebrated creator of (clean) limericks. Here are two of his best:

> I wish that my room had a floor;
> I don't care so much for a door;
>   But this walking around
>   Without touching the ground
> Is getting to be quite a bore.

I'd rather have fingers than toes;
I'd rather have ears than a nose;
   And as for my hair,
   I'm glad that it's there.
I'll be awfully sad when it goes.

John Galsworthy (1867-1933), who received the Nobel Prize for Literature in 1932, is credited with:

To an artist a husband named Bicket
Said, "Turn your backside, and I'll kick it.
   You have painted my wife
   In the nude to the life.
Do you think for a moment that's cricket?"

And Arnold Bennett (1867-1931), when he was asked to make a contribution to Langford Reed's *The Complete Limerick Book,* replied with:

There was a young man of Montrose
Who had pockets in none of his clothes.
   When asked by his lass
   Where he carried his brass,
He said, "Darling, I pay through the nose."

Carolyn Wells (1869-1942), who compiled *A Non-sense Anthology* and *A Whimsey Anthology* (both with chapters on limericks) as well as an entire book of limericks, was herself a master of the form. She specialized in tongue-twisters, of which this is a celebrated example:

A canner, exceedingly canny,
One morning remarked to his granny:
  "A canner can can
  Anything that he can,
But a canner can't can a can, can he?"[2]

Arthur Guiterman (1871-1943), the creator of so much of the best in light verse, also wrote:

The cautious collapsible cow
Gives milk by the sweat of her brow;
  Then under the trees
  She folds her front knees
And sinks fore and aft with a bow.

Bertrand Russell (1872-   ), philosopher, mathematician and winner of the Nobel Prize for Literature in 1950, is supposedly the author of:

2. Attributed to James H. Hubbard by J. R. Esenwein and M. E. Roberts in *The Art of Versification* (rev. ed.; Springfield, Massachusetts: Home Correspondence School, 1920). But the verse is found under Carolyn Wells' name in her own *Book of Humorous Verse,* and Louis Untermeyer in "Good Old Limericks" (*Good Housekeeping,* December, 1945) also credits Carolyn Wells.

There was a young girl of Shanghai
Who was so exceedingly shy,
    That undressing at night,
    She turned out the light
For fear of the All-Seeing Eye.

And Don Marquis (1878-1937), the beloved creator of Archy and Mehitabel, once composed:

There was a young fellow named Sydney,
Who drank till he ruined his kidney.
    It shriveled and shrank
    As he sat there and drank,
But he had a good time at it, didn't he?[3]

Oliver St. John Gogarty (1878-1957), writing in *As I Was Going Down Sackville Street,* attributed this limerick to his friend James Joyce (1882-1941):

There was a young priest named Delaney
Who said to the girls, "*Nota bene,*
    'Twould tempt the archbishop
    The way that you swish up
Your skirts when the weather is rainy."

3. Marquis once tried to put a market-place classification on limericks:

Limericks that can be told in the presence of ladies —$1.

Limericks that can be told in the presence of the clergy—$2.

LIMERICKS—$10.

And still another able versifier who had a re-markable facility with limericks was the late Ber-ton Braley (1882-1966). In 1925 Braley took part in a limerick contest with 200 other versifiers at the Roosevelt Hotel in New York City. Given the first line, he won first prize with this quick effort:

> There was an old fellow named Bryan,
> Whose voice was forevermore cryin'
>   "Do you think that my shape
>   Was derived from an ape?
> Well, I think Charlie Darwin was lyin'."

Braley could do even better when he had a little more time at his disposal:

> According to experts, the oyster
> In its shell—or crustacean cloister—
>   May frequently be
>   Either he or a she
> Or both, if it should be its choice ter.

Heywood Broun (1888-1939) created a very fa-mous limerick when he wrote:

There was a young man with a hernia
Who said to his doctor, "Goldernia,
    When improving my middle
    Be sure you don't fiddle
With matters that do not concernia."

And readers of *Eyeless in Gaza* (1936) by Aldous
Huxley (1894-1963) will recall that he quoted the
opening lines of two limericks which he may also
have created:

There was a young fellow of Burma
Whose betrothed had good reason to murmur.
    But now that he's married he's
    Been using cantharides
And the root of their love is much firmer.

There was a young girl of East Anglia
Whose loins were a tangle of ganglia.
    Her mind was a webbing
    Of Freud and Krafft-Ebing
And all sorts of other new-fanglia.

Aubrey Beardsley

Aubrey Beardsley

Even poets of the caliber of T. S. Eliot (1888-1965) and W. H. Auden (1907-   ) have not scorned the lowly limerick.

Eliot paraphrased a well-known limerick of questionable taste in these lines from his poem *The Waste Land:*

> O the moon shines bright on Mrs. Porter
> And on her daughter
> They wash their feet in soda water . . .

And Auden's most recent creation, published in *The New York Review of Books* (May 12, 1966), goes:

> The Marquis de Sade and Genet
> Are most highly thought of today;
>   But torture and treachery
>   Are not my sort of lechery,
> So I've given my copies away.

Nor should we forget Edward Gorey and his book of limericks of a few years ago, *The Listing Attic.* Clifton Fadiman has found these limericks "so appalling that I prefer not to quote them here. . . .

Aubrey Beardsley

MESSALINA.

Aubrey Beardsley

Mr. Gorey thinks nothing of wrapping up such material as infanticide, simple murder, algolagnia, human vivisection, and the lynching of sexual deviants in a verse form traditionally consecrated to the innocent enjoyments of the nursery."

But Mr. Gorey displays much wit and high rhyming ingenuity:

> From Number Nine, Penwiper Mews,
> There is really abominable news:
>   They've discovered a head
>   In the box for the bread
> But nobody seems to know whose.

Still, Morris Bishop (1893-   ) and Ogden Nash (1902-   ), for years two of our most brilliant light versifiers, have also experimented widely with the limerick form and are generally considered to be its modern masters.

Here is one of Mr. Bishop's limericks from the twenty-nine collected in *Spilt Milk:*

> There's a tiresome young man from Bay Shore;
> When his fiancée cried, "I adore

The beautiful sea!"
He replied, "I agree
It's pretty. But what is it *for?*"

Of Mr. Nash's many limericks, the most quoted
is probably "The Young Belle of Old Natchez,"
from *The Face Is Familiar:*

There was a young girl of old Natchez
Whose garments were always in patchez.
    When comment arose
    On the state of her clothes,
She drawled, "When Ah itchez, Ah scratchez."

Even more recently, in 1964, Conrad Aiken (1889-
    ), poet, novelist and Pulitzer Prize winner, has
beguiled a term in the hospital by devising fifty-
one limericks that have now been published in a
little book called *A Seizure of Limericks.* (Commented Morris Bishop, "*Seizure* is good; a mild
taste for limericks can lead to seizures, addiction,
septic logorrhea and compulsive recitation neu-
roses.") Here is Mr. Aiken on the limerick:

André Domin

The limerick's, admitted, a verse form:
A terse form: a curse form: a hearse form.
　　It may not be lyric
　　And at best its Satyric,
And a whale of a tail in perverse form.

Statesmen as well as writers—ambassadors, vice presidents and at least one President of the United States—have had their fun with this "terse form." Joseph Kennedy (1888-   ), father of the late President Kennedy, wrote shortly after the Treaty of Versailles ended World War I:

Says the Frenchman, "You'll pay us for sure."
Says the German, "We can't for we're poor."
　　So Fritz with a whine
　　Sings his "Watch on the Rhine,"
But the Poilu sings, "Watch on the Ruhr."

Vice President Alben Barkley (1877-1956) was the creator of:

In New Orleans dwelled a young Creole
Who, when asked if her hair was all reole,

Replied with a shrug
"Just give it a tug
And decide by the way that I squeole."

And President Woodrow Wilson (1856-1924) was
so fond of quoting one limerick in particular that
many people think he wrote it:

As a beauty I'm not a great star,
There are others more handsome by far,
But my face, I don't mind it,
Because I'm behind it—
'Tis the folks in the front that I jar.[4]

With more justification, Wilson has been credited with the authorship of another limerick, and
it is a gem:

I sat next to the Duchess at tea;
It was just as I feared it would be:
Her rumblings abdominal
Were truly phenomenal,
And everyone thought it was me!

4. Actually, this limerick was the work of a minor
poet named Anthony Euwer, and part of a sequence
which Euwer called *The Limeratomy*, a word which
combines "limerick" with "anatomy." As Euwer ex-
plained it:

As I lay in my bed on the flat o' me,
I was shocked at the sight of the fat o' me,
So to keep my nerves steady
I concocted and edi-
ted this luminous, lim'rick anatomy.

Here are two others in the sequence—Euwer on "The
Hands" and "The Smile":

The hands, they were made to assist
In supplying the features with grist.
    There are only a few—
    As a rule about two—
And are hitched to the end of the wrist.

No matter how grouchy you're feeling,
You'll find the smile more or less healing.
    It grows in a wreath
    All around the front teeth—
Thus preserving the face from congealing.

Aubrey Beardsley

André Domin

VII *The Limerick, Unlaundered:*

"There was a young girl of Aberystwith . . ."

André Domin

FOR EVERY FAD, there is an anti-fad.

Certainly this was true of the fad of the clean limerick.

Alfred, Lord Tennyson (1809-92) is supposed to have written many fine erotic limericks, perhaps as a release from composing the saccharine stanzas of his *Idylls of the King* (1859; enlarged 1869, 1872); but all of them were destroyed soon after his death.

The real leader of the rebellion against the fad of the pure limerick would seem to have been the poet Algernon Charles Swinburne (1837-1909), whose collected works leave uncollected his sub-rosa poetry and erotic prose, including the classic limerick:

> There was a young girl of Aberystwyth
> Who took grain to the mill to get grist with.
>   The miller's son, Jack,
>   Laid her flat on her back
> And united the organs they pissed with.

Almost inevitably, Swinburne and his followers opened the attack by parodying the limericks of Lear. The inoffensive "Young Lady from Norway Who Casually Sat in a Doorway" became:

There was a young lady of Norway
Who hung by her toes in a doorway.
    She said to her beau:
    "Just look at me, Joe,
I think I've discovered one more way."

The "Old Man of Cape Horn, Who Wished He Had Never Been Born" was translated into:

There was a young man of Cape Horn
Who wished he had never been born;
    And he wouldn't have been
    If his father had seen
That the end of the rubber was torn.[1]

Lear's "Old Man of Dundee," who was content with frequenting the top of a tree was transformed into:

There was an old man of Dundee
Who molested an ape in a tree:
    The result was most horrid,
    All arse and no forehead,
Three balls and a purple goatee.[2]

[1] Norman Douglas included this as the final limerick in his collection, *Some Limericks,* and appended a facetious "annotation" which reads in part:

I should apologise for inserting this well-known lyric but for the fact that so perfect a specimen of the Golden Period cannot be excluded from a collection like this. The smoothness of the versification: the glamour that hangs about mysterious regions like Tierra del Fuego: the wistfulness of the opening lines and the anticlimax of the last one—they all testify to the genius of the Unknown Poet.

[2] There is also the innocent:

. . . young lass from Dundee,
Whose knowledge of French was *"Oui, oui."*
    When they asked *"Parlez vous?"*
    She replied, "Same to you"—
A fine bit of fast *repartee.*

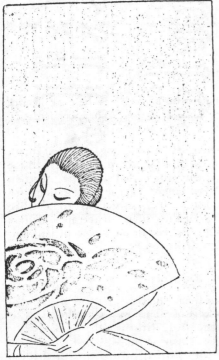

André Domin

The "Young Lady of Greenwich, Whose Garments Were Bordered with Spinach" was metamorphosed into:

There once was a young man of Greenwich
Whose balls were all covered with spinach;
    So long was his tool
    That it wound round a spool
And he let it out inach by inach.

A. C. Hilton's "Young Gourmand of Johns" suffered a like fate:

There was a young student of Johns
Who wanted to bugger the swans.
    But the loyal hall porter
    Said, "Sir, take my daughter.
Them birds are reserved for the dons."

Without much doubt, the greatest living authority on the bawdy limerick is the folklorist Gershon (originally George Alexander) Legman. In his scholarly but highly readable essay, "The Limerick: A History in Brief," in *The Horn Book,* Legman summarizes the publishing history of the limerick as an indecent verse form.

According to Legman, then, the earliest collection of erotic limericks known to have existed was the twelve-page *A New Book of Nonsense* (London, 1868), no trace of which has survived "except a bare reference to its title, in the important Campbell-Reddie manuscript bibliography of nineteenth-century erotica (II. 175)."

Very shortly afterwards, however, there appeared a collection tastefully titled *Cythera's Hymnal, or Flakes from the Foreskin,* under the mock imprint, "Oxford: Printed at the University Press, for the Society for Promoting Useful Knowledge" (really London, 1870). "It must be admitted," says Legman, "that this is one of the least pleasant and least readable such volumes that has ever been printed." In the main, it is a collection of songs and poems of the (early) music hall variety, but it also includes a group of fifty-one erotic limericks, headed "Nursery Rhymes." *Cythera's Hymnal* is attributed to Captain Edward Sellon, an erotic novelist of the

1860's, and the journalist, George Augustus Sala, also the author of an erotic playlet titled *Harlequin Prince Cherrytop* (sometimes known as *The Sod's Opera* and attributed, quite falsely, to Gilbert and Sullivan).

This was followed by an extraordinary magazine called *The Pearl,* which ran for eighteen consecutive months in 1879-80, and was continued by a publication called *The Cremorne.* To *The Pearl* and *The Cremorne* we owe a new grouping of sixty-five bawdy limericks.

In our own times, however, by far the most widely-known collections of erotic and scatological limericks are those inoffensively-titled volumes called *Some Limericks* and *The Limerick.*

Some Limericks is the collection and in part the creation of the Scottish antiquarian (*London Street Games,* 1913-16) and stylistic novelist Norman Douglas, whose love affair with the island of Capri he celebrated in *South Wind* (1917). *Some Limericks*—there are only sixty-eight of them—was originally published in Florence by G. Oriolo in 1928. It has been reprinted in New York (Guy d'Isère for David Moss, 1928), in Philadelphia (1931), in Paris

(Obelisk Press, 1939), and in Boston (Nicholson and Whitney, 1942). (The first American edition is currently being offered at $40 a copy.)

The Limerick, the closest thing to a "definitive" collection of bawdy limericks that has ever appeared, or is likely to appear, was published in Paris in 1953. It is a tome of more than five hundred pages and contains nearly eighteen hundred classic examples of the form. They stem, mainly, from some twenty printed sources dating from 1870 (*Cythera's Hymnal*) to 1949 (*A Book of Anglo-Saxon Verse*). The rest are principally from oral collections made in Ann Arbor, Michigan; in Berkeley, California; and in New York.

Nowhere in his essay on "The Limerick" does Legman acknowledge that he himself is the compiler of *The Limerick* (he also contributed several original limericks to it), but such is the fact, as has several times appeared in print, notably in Martin Gardner's notes to C. C. Bombaugh's *Oddities and Curiosities of Words and Literature.* Gardner should know: He is a personal friend of Legman's.

Since so little has appeared about Legman in the American press, except for brief mentions in *Time,*

Aubrey Beardsley

The New Yorker, and the book columns of *The New York Times* and the *New York Herald Tribune,* it may be well to summarize here the biographical information which appears on the jacket of *The Horn Book:*

Born in Scranton, Pennsylvania, 45 years ago [1917], Legman has lived on the French Riviera for the last fifteen years, in an old, partially restored installation of the Knights Templar; he has managed, in the last two years, to introduce piped water into his ex-monastery but doubts if he will attain the mixed twentieth-century blessing of central heating. When not engaged in writing, he tends his olive orchard.

Mr. Legman's life has also included a period as official bibliographer for the Kinsey Institute, and he is credited with being the first to introduce the Japanese folk-art of origami (paper-folding) to the United States. A noted lecturer and writer, he has been editor of *Neurotica* magazine; is the author of *Love & Death: A Study in Censorship* (1949), now in its second

edition; and has written many other works, both publicly and privately printed . . .

Both Douglas' *Some Limericks* and Legman's *The Limerick* have been shamelessly plagiarized: *Some Limericks* by "Nosti" in *A Collection of Limericks,* issued in Switzerland in 1944 and fortunately very rare; and *The Limerick* by "Count Palmiro Vicarion"[3] in his *Book of Limericks,* issued in Paris in 1955.

There is also the volume called *From Bed to Verse,* printed secretly in Wiesbaden in 1945 by some members of the Army of Occupation in Germany: the one copy your editor is sure exists (and that is a damaged copy) is in the Beinecke Rare Book and Manuscript Library at Yale.

According to Legman, there is only one "really interesting continuation" of the Douglas-Legman line: *That Immortal Garland,* "an original manuscript by the American poet and translator . . . C. F. MacIntyre, which includes over a hundred of this poet's original bawdy limericks, of which he is justly proud; not one of which begins with the inactive 'There *was* . . .' but leaps incontinently into

3. Or "Vicarrion," identified, Legman writes, "in recent catalogues of the British bookseller Bernard Stone, as the internationally famous Liverpool poet, Mr. Christopher Logue, whose own signed volumes of Angry Young Man (British beatnik) poetry have been compared by *Time* magazine to the *Song of Songs.* I would not go quite so far."

André Domin

the action of the piece from the very first line on . . ."

More recently, however (1966), a paperbound book titled *Grand Prix Limerix: 1001 New Limericks You Never Saw Before* has been published in Fort Worth. The author, who prefers to remain anonymous, is a San Francisco account executive and copy writer who claims in his Foreword to have written "no less than the staggering total of *ten thousand raunchy limericks, and another ten thousand clean!* (The present thousand-and-one are a combination of both.)" Another volume is promised.

So much for the publishing history, to date, of the limerick, unlaundered.

Before we close this chapter, however, we should answer the question: What makes a limerick "unlaundered"?

Two things, of course:

First, its subject matter. This is perhaps best exemplified by listing the chapter headings in *The Limerick* (themselves borrowed from *Lapses in Limerick*, an oral collection made in Ann Arbor, Michigan): Little Romances, Organs, Strange In-

tercourse, Oral Irregularity, Buggery, Abuses of the
Clergy, Zoophily, Excrement, Gourmands, Virginity, Motherhood, Prostitution, Diseases, Losses, Sex
Substitutes, Assorted Eccentricities, Weak Sisters,
and Chamber of Horrors.

Second, its use of pungent four-letter (for the
most part) words, which A. Reynolds Morse, the
compiler of *The Limerick: A Facet of Our Culture,*
calls "the maypoles of limerology around which
lesser words perform a merry dance."

Here, from the just-mentioned book, is an "Ode
to Four-Letter Words," very popular in the 1940's:
it is doggerel, and pretty dreary doggerel at that,
but it will provide an opportunity to comment:

> Banish the use of the four-letter words
> Whose meanings are never obscure.
> The Angles and Saxons, those bawdy old birds,
> Were vulgar, obscene and impure.
> But cherish the use of the weak-kneed phrase
> That never quite says what you mean;
> You'd better be known for your hypocrite ways
> Than as vulgar, impure or obscene.

Aubrey Beardsley

When nature is calling, plain speaking is out.
When ladies, God bless 'em, are milling about,
You may wee-wee, make water, or empty the
      glass;
You can powder your nose; even "Johnnie"
      may pass;
Shake the dew off the lily, see the man 'bout the
      dog,
Or when everyone's soused, it's "condensing
      the fog."
But be pleased to remember if you would
      know bliss
That only in Shakespeare do characters – – – –.

As a noun or as a verb, the word omitted here
has been considered a vulgarism since around 1760.
It probably originated as an "echoic" word. *"Ah, si
je pouvais pisser comme il parle,"* Clemenceau once
said of Lloyd George. As an example of modern
mores, the editor can cite a conversation he had recently with a comely young matron in a sophisti-
cated northern suburb of New York City. "I don't
object to the word 'pee,' " she said, "because that's
something my own children do. But 'piss' is for

truckdrivers." Was there a latent memory here, perhaps, of the limerick about "Dear Lady Norris"?

" 'Tis my custom," said dear Lady Norris,
"To beg lifts from the drivers of lorries.
 When they get out to piss
 I see things that I miss
At the wheel of my two-seater Morris."

To continue:

When your dinners are hearty with onions and
 beans,
With garlic and claret and bacon and greens;
Your bowels get busy distilling a gas
That Nature insists be permitted to pass.
You are very polite, and try to exhale
Without noise or odor (you frequently fail);
Expecting a zephyr, you usually start,
For even a deafer would call it a – – – –.

The word goes back to the thirteenth century, at
least, and it was used by both Chaucer in "The

Miller's Tale" ("He was somdel squaymous of fart-ing") and Jonson in *The Alchemist* ("I fart at thee"). In 1731, in his "Strephon and Chloë," Swift warned parents that this habit is notorious for its stifling effect on romance.

> You may speak of a "movement" or sit on a
>   seat,
> Have a passage, or stool—or simply excrete,
> Or say to the others, "I'm going out in back"
> And groan in pure joy in that smelly old shack.
> You can go "lay a cable" or "do number two"
> Or sit on the toidey and make a "do-do,"
> But ladies and men who are socially fit
> Under no provocation will go take a – – – –.

A fifteenth-century word, a vulgarism since the nineteenth century. "Before [World War I] didn't you sportsmen call everybody who didn't hunt or shoot by a very coarse name, which we can change euphemistically into—squirts?", H. A. Vachell wrote in his *The Disappearance of Martha Penny* (1934).

A woman has bosoms, a bust or a breast,
Those lily-white swellings that bulge 'neath
    her vest.
They are towers of ivory, sheaves of new wheat;
In a moment of passion, ripe apples to eat.
You may speak of her nipples as small rings of
    fire
With hardly a question of raising her ire,
But by Rabelais' beard will she throw fits
If you speak of them roundly as good honest
    – – – –.

A solecism for "teats," probably first used in
the seventeenth century or earlier. Despite the
warning voiced just above, we cannot resist the
temptation to bring you here:

To his bride said the lynx-eyed detective,
"Can it be that my eyesight's defective?
    Has your east tit the least bit
    The best of the west tit?
Or is it a trick of perspective?"

It's a cavern of joy you are thinking of now,
A warm, tender field just waiting the plow.

André Domin

It's a quivering pigeon, caressing your hand,
Or the National Anthem that makes us all
 stand.
Or perhaps it's a flower, a grotto, a well,
The hope of the world, or a velvety hell,
But friend heed this warning, beware the af-
 front
Of aping a Saxon: don't call it a − − − −.

The word stems from the Latin *cuneus,* a wedge.
Since the fifteenth century, it has been avoided in
polite spoken English. Eric Partridge in his *Dictionary of Slang and Unconventional English* (New
York: The Macmillan Company, 1961) calls it "perhaps the most notable of all vulgarisms." Since
around 1700 it has, except in the reprinting of old
classics, been held to be obscene; that is, it is a legal
offense to print it in full. Says Partridge: "Had the
late Sir James Murray courageously included the
word and spelt it in full, in the great *Oxford English Dictionary* the situation would be different; as
it is, neither the *Universal Dictionary of English*
(1932) nor the *Shorter Oxford Dictionary* (1933)

Aubrey Beardsley

had the courage to include it. (Yet the O. E. D. gave
prick: why this . . . injustice to women?"

> Though a lady repel your advance, she'll be
>   kind
> Just as long as you "intimate" what's on your
>   mind.
> You may tell her you're hungry, you need to be
>   swung,
> You may ask her to see how your etchings are
>   hung.
> You may mention the ashes that need to be
>   hauled;
> Put the lid on her sauce-pan ("lay" isn't too
>   bald);
> But the moment you're forthright, get ready to
>   duck:
> The girl isn't born yet who'll stand for "Let's
>   – – – –."

The latest dictionary to include the word would
seem to be Grose's *Dictionary of the Vulgar Tongue*
(1823). Shakespeare, Fletcher, Urquhart, D'Urfey

André Domin

and Burns all used the word in one form or another, but the recent efforts of James Joyce and D. H. Lawrence to put it back into literary standing have not restored it to its original dignified status.

> So banish the words that Elizabeth used,
> When she was a Queen on her throne.
> The modern maid's virtue is easily bruised
> By the four-letter words when used all alone.
> Let your morals be loose as an alderman's vest
> As long as the language you use is obscure:
> Today not the *act* but the *word* is the test
> Of the vulgar, obscene and impure.

There are two other four-letter words which sober reflection demands that we bar from this book. Both are vulgarisms for the female pudendum. The first perhaps stems from the Spanish *quemar,* to burn. But the obscure English verb *queme* provides, variously, less irritating possibilities: the word can mean to please, gratify, satisfy, appease, mitigate, slip in, join or fit closely. Partridge tells us that our second word was used by the poet Robert Browning (1812-89) in his poem "Pippa Passes" "by a hair-raising misapprehension—the literary world's worst 'brick.' " (Browning thought it denoted some part of a nun's attire.) It is derived from *twachylle* or *twitchel,* a passage, and the dialectic *twatch,* to mend a gap in a hedge.

Again, before we close this chapter, we should refer to an important point first put forward by Professor Weston LaBarre, writing in the journal *Psychiatry* in 1939, and commented upon by both Legman and the editors of *Eros:* that limericks are written and retailed *only* by the educated group. Legman adds:

> Limericks are not only the folklore of the educated, but are almost their only folklore, with the exception of jokes and tales—including a large number credulously believed to be true—and a limited repertoire of bawdy and sentimental songs. . . . It is obvious that the ordinary cowboy, miner, fieldhand or working-

Aubrey Beardsley

man will not go for effects and over-intellec-
tual stuff . . . in either Britain or America. The
workingman, in such a mood, prefers singing
"The One-Eyed Riley" or " 'Twas on the Good
Ship *Venus*" or "The Bastard King of England" or "The Crab Fish," when he does any
singing at all, or is *allowed* to sing—even polite songs—in his public bar . . .

LYSISTRATA

Aubrey Beardsley

VIII *"The Best Limericks of All"*:

The Young Lady of Riga and

the Young Plumber of Leigh

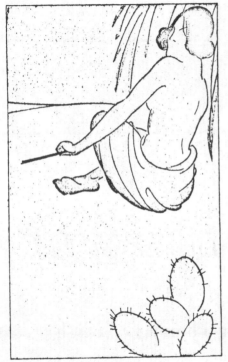

Aubrey Beardsley

By WRITING to dozens of his correspondents, Langford Reed in 1925 made a valiant effort to determine "The Best Limerick of All."

In the nursery-clean field of the form, the winner was overwhelmingly the famous "Young Lady of Riga":

> There was a young lady of Riga
> Who smiled as she rode on a tiger;
> > They returned from the ride
> > With the lady inside,
> And the smile on the face of the tiger.

A writer to *The Referee* once complained that the version given here must be a misquotation, "firstly because there are no tigers in Riga, and secondly because Riga doesn't rhyme with tiger. It was, of course, a young lady from Niger who sailed forth on that interesting but fatal excursion."

But Reed stood firm for "Riga." He replied that the first objection "is balanced by the fact that there are no tigers in Africa, either; and the second circumvented by reason of the Riga version having been the correct and classic form of the

limerick ever since it became one—about seventy
years ago. The author has seen a 'puzzle card' containing it, dated 1873."[1]

Arnold Bennett, however, gave a very different
answer to Reed's difficult question. Bennett chose
the "Young Plumber of Leigh," but gave Reed only
the first line, adding, "Unfortunately I am pre-
cluded from putting this chef d'oeuvre upon record for the reason that it is unprintable."
Here is Bennett's "unprintable" limerick:

> There was a young plumber of Leigh
> Was plumbing a maid by the sea.
> Said the maid, "Cease your plumbing,
> I think someone's coming."
> Said the plumber, still plumbing, "It's me."[2]

If "The Young Lady of Riga" is the best (clean)
limerick of all, the previously mentioned William
Cosmo Monkhouse and the veteran Florida news-
paperman, Dixon Merritt, have certainly created
two to rival it. Respectively, they are:

1. Louis Untermeyer has nevertheless attributed "The
Young Lady of Riga" to William Cosmo Monkhouse, a
witty Englishman who was primarily a commentator on
art. Monkhouse wrote many fine limericks, but we doubt
that he wrote "the best limerick of all."

2. There is also the pseudo-Gallic version:

> There was a young plumber from Pau
> Was plumbing a maid in the Bois.
> Said the maid, "Cease your plumbing,
> I think someone's coming."
> Said the plumber, still plumbing, *"C'est moi."*

There once was an old man of Lyme
Who married three wives at a time;
 When asked "Why a third?"
 He replied, "One's absurd!
And bigamy, sir, is a crime."

And:

A rare old bird is the pelican;
His bill holds more than his belican.
 He can take in his beak
 Enough food for a week;
I'm darned if I know how the helican!

Whether or not these are, in truth, "the best limericks of all," the reader will soon have a chance to judge for himself in the collection of personal favorites—laundered and unlaundered—which follows. (The limericks have been grouped from A to Z, alphabetized by the first rhyme word, to make it easy for anyone to locate his favorite limericks speedily.) But here let us sound a note of caution. We are in full agreement with the man who signs himself "Count Palmiro Vicarion" when he writes

in the Foreword to his *Book of Limericks:* "... the limerick is precious, an exquisite thing; like a good Burgundy, it should not be taken indifferently, too often, or in unduly large quantities. Only a fool, I repeat, a fool would gulp down a glass of Chambertin or read this book in a sitting ..."

Lastly, let us consider briefly the limerick in the world of "only yesterday" and today, and its future in the world of tomorrow.

When H. I. Brock wrote an article called "A Century of Limericks" for *The New York Times Magazine Section* of November 17, 1946, the paper was flooded with verses sent in by readers and only three weeks later (December 8, 1946) published many of them in a "Limerick Addenda."

Much more recently, your editor has attended meetings of a New York City luncheon club, composed entirely of highly literate business and professional men, who profess that their organization has two purposes only: first, to prove that Shakespeare wrote Shakespeare, and nobody else;[3] second, to collect and card-file in their archives every erotic limerick known to English-speaking man.

3. Not even, as Mark Twain once said, "another man *of the same name.*"

André Domin

Limericks can still be heard *sung* (as in Limerick, Ireland, so many years ago?) at the dinners of college fraternities and the drinking clubs of Army, Navy and Air Force officers, and an earnest effort to create and publish new and original limericks (not all of them *risqué,* by any means) is now being made by The Poets Club of New York City in their (more or less) monthly newssheet, *The Poets,* edited by Ward Byron.

Collections of limericks, not erotic but certainly sprightly, are now being offered for sale quite openly by the better paperback bookstores at $1.00 a copy or less: to mention only two, there are: *Laundered Limericks,* published by the respected Peter Pauper Press of Mount Vernon, New York, in 1960 (much more lively than any of the previous Peter Pauper collections); and *Limericks for the John,* by George Gordon and Lawrence Eisenberg, published in New York by Kanrom, Inc., in 1963. (This little book of forty-two limericks comes complete with a chain by which it may be hung in the appropriate room.)

The limerick, then, is a living thing. And with

the college-educated population of the United States growing yearly by leaps and bounds, the limerick can be said to have a future and a bright one.

And now let us see if we can sum up in a paragraph what many commentators have tried to express about the total scope of the limerick at its best:

It embraces every topic, territory and temperament. It absorbs solemnities and absurdities, traditional legends and off-color jokes, devout reflections and downright indecencies. Geography is its happy hunting ground, but matters vegetable, animal and mineral are all grist to its merry mill. Love of all kinds is fair game; bishops and tomcats are equally its targets. In politics, divinity, philosophy, philology, zoology; in botany, relativity, revelry and ribaldry the limerick is equally at home. All the follies, foibles, fortunes, failures and fallacies to which mortal flesh is heir, from the cradle to the grave, are the stuff to which its antics give the *coup de pied . . .*

Aubrey Beardsley

PART TWO:

THE LIMERICK FROM A TO Z

A: *"A famous theatrical actress . . ."*

A famous theatrical actress
Played best in the role of malefactress;
    Yet her home life was pure
    Except, to be sure,
A scandal or two just for practice.

In the Garden of Eden lay Adam
Complacently stroking his madam,
    And loud was his mirth
    For he knew that on earth
There were only two balls—and he had 'em.

The Rajah of Afghanistan
Imported a Birmingham can
    Which he set as a throne
    On a great Buddha stone—
But he crapped out of doors like a man.[1]

A sculptor remarked, "I'm afraid
I have fallen in love with my trade.
    I'm much too elated
    With what I've created,
And, chiefly, the women I've made."

1. Compare:

    The parish commission at Roylette
    Bought their vicar a pristine new toilet.
        But he still voids his bowels
        On a heap of old towels,
    He's so reluctant to soil it.

There is a young lady named Aird
Whose bottom is always kept bared;
    When asked why, she pouts,
    And says the Boy Scouts
All beg her to please Be Prepared.

Said the mythical King of Algiers
To his harem assembled, "My dears,
    You may think it odd of me
    But I'm tired of sodomy;
Tonight's for you ladies." (*Loud cheers.*)[2]

There was a young lady named Alice
Who peed in a Catholic chalice.
    The Padre agreed
    'Twas done out of need,
And not out of Protestant malice.[3]

An old maid in the land of Aloha
Got wrapped in the coils of a boa;
    And as the snake squeezed,
    The old maid, not displeased,
Cried: "Darling! I love it! Samoa!"

2. Norman Douglas attributes this to a trilogy, of which another stanza goes:

> Then up spoke the King of Siam:
> "For women I don't give a damn.
>   But a round-bottomed boy
>   Is my pride and my joy.
> They call me a bugger—I am!"

3. The psychological significance of the limerick, particularly the bawdy limerick, as an outlet for aggressions has long been recognized, and the reader should not be too shocked to find in this collection many limericks straining against the authority of the Church and lampooning Churchmen as grossly lewd and corrupt. This tradition the limerick shares with the nursery rhyme—as we have pointed out in a previous book (*The Annotated Mother Goose,* compiled in collaboration with Ceil Baring-Gould; New York: Clarkson N. Potter, Inc., 1962).

Aubrey Beardsley

A charmer from old Amarillo,
Sick of finding strange heads on her pillow,
    Decided one day
    That to keep men away
She would stuff up her crevice with Brillo.

A sleeper from the Amazon
Put nighties of his gra'mazon—
    The reason: That
    He was too fat
To get his own pajamazon.

Exuberant Sue from Anjou
Found that fucking affected her hue;
    She presented to sight
    Some parts pink, some parts white,
And others quite purple and blue.

A lady there was in Antigua
Who said to her spouse, "What a pigua."
    He answered, "My queen,
    Is it manners you mean?
Or do you refer to my figua?"

An amorous maiden antique
Locked a man in her house for a week;
    He entered her door
    With a shout and a roar
But his exit was marked by a squeak.

A two-toothed old man of Arbroath
Gave vent to a terrible oath.
    When one tooth chanced to ache,
    By an awful mistake,
The dentist extracted them both.[4]

There was a young man of Atlanta,
Fell in love with a girl full of banter;
    "I should just like to see
    The man who'd make me,"
She remarked—and he made her instanter.

There was a young man from Australia
Who painted his ass like a dahlia.
    The color was fine;
    Likewise the design;
The aroma—ah, that was a failia.[5]

4. And, speaking of extractions, the following limerick, by Richard H. Field, extracted an answer from Frederick Winsor. Both limericks appear in David McCord's sparkling collection of humorous verse, *What Cheer!:*

When you go to a store in Ascutney,
There is no use to ask them for chutney.
    You may plea, you may tease,
    You may go on your knees:
It will do you no good, they ain't got any.

At the village emporium in Woodstock
Of chutney they keep quite a good stock;
    They're more given to gluttony
    Than the folk of Ascutney
Who neither of liquors or foods talk.

5. Some may prefer:

There was a young girl from Australia
Who went to a dance as a dahlia.
    When the petals uncurled
    They revealed to the world
That as clothing the dress was a failia

B: *"There was a young fellow named Baker . . ."*

André Domin

There was a young fellow named Baker,
Who seduced a vivacious young Quaker.
    And when he had done it,
    She straightened her bonnet,
And said: "I give thanks to my maker."

A lassie from wee Ballachulish
Observed, "Och, virginity's foolish;
    When a lad makes a try,
    To say ought but 'Aye!'
Is stubborn, pig-headed, and mulish."

A bather in Lake Ballyclear
Had a bust that would burst a brassière;
    She had a round face,
    And was plump everyplace,
Except for her flat-chested rear.

There was a young lady of Bandon,
Whose feet were too narrow to stand on;
    So she stood on her head,
    "For my motto," she said,
"Has always been *Nil desperandum*."

A daring young fellow in Bangor
Sneaked a super-swift jet from its hangar.
    When he crashed in the bay,
    Neighbors laid him away
In rather more sorrow than anger.

There was a young girl of Baroda
Who built an erotic pagoda;
    The walls of its halls
    Were festooned with the balls
And the tools of the fools who bestrode her.

There was a young sailor named Bates
Who danced the fandango on skates,
    But a fall on his cutlass
    Rendered him nutless,
And practically useless on dates.

A buxom young typist named Baynes
At her work took particular pains.
    She was good at dictation
    And long explanations,
But she ran more to bosom than brains.

André Domin

On a maiden a man once begat
Bouncing triplets named Nat, Tat, and Pat;
 'Twas fun in the breeding
 But hell in the feeding:
She hadn't a spare tit for Tat.

God's plan made a hopeful beginning
But man spoiled his chances by sinning.
 We trust that the story
 Will end in God's glory,
But at present the other side's winning.

There was a young man from Belgrave
Who kept a dead whore in a cave.
 He said, "I admit
 I'm a bit of a shit,
But think of the money I save."

There's a young man who lives in Belsize
Who believes he is clever and wise.
 Now, what do you think?
 He saves gallons of ink
By simply not dotting his i's.

A nudist resort in Benares
Took a midget in all unawares.
    But he made members weep
    For he just couldn't keep
His nose out of private affairs.

There was a young man of Bengal
Who went to a masquerade ball
    Arrayed like a tree,
    But he failed to foresee
His abuse by the dogs in the hall.

There once was a person of Benin,
Who wore clothes not fit to be seen in;
    When told that he shouldn't,
    He replied, "Gumscrumrudent!"—
A word of inscrutable meanin'![1]

There was a young man from Berlin
Whose tool was the size of a pin.
    Said his girl with a laugh
    As she fondled his shaft,
"Well, *this* won't be much of a sin."

1. One of the many fine limericks attributed to Cosmo Monkhouse.

I met a lewd nude in Bermuda,
Who thought she was shrewd; I was shrewder;
    She thought it quite crude
    To be wooed in the nude;
I pursued her, subdued her, and screwed her.

A lisping young lady named Beth
Was saved from a fate worse than death
    Seven times in a row,
    Which unsettled her so,
That she quit saying "No" and said "Yeth."

"I shall star," vowed a girl from Biloxi,
"At Twentieth-Century-Foxi,"
    And her movie career
    Really prospered last year:
She's in charge of the mops at the Roxi.

There was a young parson named Bings,
Who talked about God and such things;
    But his secret desire
    Was a boy in the choir,
With a bottom like jelly on springs.

There were two young ladies of Birmingham,
And this is the story concerning 'em:
    They lifted the frock
    And diddled the cock
Of the Bishop as he was confirming 'em.[2]

There once was a hardened old bitch
With a motorized self-frigger which
    She would use with delight
    Far into the night—
Twenty bucks—Abercrombie & Fitch.

There was an old man of Blackheath,
Who sat on his set of false teeth;
    Said he, with a start,
    "Oh, Lord bless my heart!
I have bitten myself underneath!"[3]

There was a young fellow named Bliss
Whose sex life was strangely amiss.
    For even with Venus
    His recalcitrant penis
Would seldom do better than t
        h
        i
        s.

2. This, one of the most celebrated of bawdy limericks, has a lesser-known, coupled sequel:

The Bishop was nobody's fool—
He'd been to a large public school;
    He took down his britches
    And diddled those bitches
With a twelve-inch Episcopal tool.

But that didn't bother those two;
They said as the Bishop withdrew:
    "Oh, the Vicar is quicker
    And thicker and slicker
And longer and stronger than you."

3. Or:

An accident really uncanny
Befell a respectable granny;
    She sat down in a chair
    While her false teeth were there,
And bit herself right in the fanny.

There once was a fellow named Bob
Who in sexual ways was a snob.
　　　One day he went swimmin'
　　　With twelve naked women
And deserted them all for a gob.

There was a young fellow from Boise
Who at times was exceedingly noise;
　　　So his friends' joy increased
　　　When he moved way back east
To what people in Brooklyn call Joise.[4]

A pathetic old maid of Bordeaux
Fell in love with a dashing young beau.
　　　To arrest his regard
　　　She would squat in his yard
And appealingly pee in the snow.

A young trapeze artist named Bract
Is faced by a very sad fact.
　　　Imagine his pain
　　　When, again and again,
He catches his wife in the act!

4. This ingenious limerick is by John Straley.

An indolent vicar of Bray
His roses allowed to decay.
   His wife, more alert,
    Bought a powerful squirt
And said to her spouse, "Let us spray."[5]

A maiden at college named Breeze,
Weighed down by B. A.'s and Litt. D.'s,
   Collapsed from the strain.
    Alas, it was plain
She was killing herself by degrees.

There once was a fellow named Brett
Loved a girl in his shiny Corvette;
   We know it's absurd
    But the last that we heard
They hadn't untangled them yet.[6]

A delighted incredulous bride
Remarked to the groom at her side:
   "I never could quite
    Believe till tonight
Our anatomies *would* coincide."

5. This limerick is one of the most constantly quoted and misquoted. It is rarely credited to anyone. Its author, however, was Langford Reed, the sponsor and strongest supporter of the Limerick, Ireland, theory of the origin of the name "limerick."

6. One of a series of limericks that might be termed "auto-erotic":

A fellow from old Copenhagen
Wooed a girl in his little Volkswagen;
   But the damage was high:
    The stick-shift in his eye,
And a gash from the dash in his noggin'.

A guy with a girl in a Fiat
Asked, "Where on earth is my key at?"
   When he started to seek
    She let out a shriek:
"That's *not* where it's likely to be at!"

They sat in his little old Lloyd
Frustrated, and hot, and annoyed;
   But enough of palaver:
    He attempted to have 'er
And the car was entirely destroyed.

Said a man of his small Morris Minor:
"For petting, it couldn't be finer;
    But for love's consummation
    A wagon called station
Would offer a playground diviner."

7. The habits of rabbits are famed in erotic folklore:

The thoughts of the rabbit on sex
Are seldom, if ever, complex;
    For a rabbit in need
    Is a rabbit indeed,
And does just as a person expects.

There was a brave damsel of Brighton
Whom nothing could possibly frighten.
    She plunged in the sea
    And with infinite glee
Was pinched by a playful old Triton.

In Boston a sub-deb named Brooks
Had a hobby of reading sex books.
    She married a Cabot
    Who looked like a rabbit
And deftly lived up to his looks.[7]

An Argentine gaucho named Bruno
Once said, "There is one thing I do know:
    A woman is fine
    And a sheep is divine,
But a llama is Numero Uno!"

There was a young lady of Brussels
Whose pride was her vaginal muscles;
    She could easily plex them
    And so interflex them
As to whistle love songs through her bustles.

There was a plump girl from Bryn Mawr
Who committed a dreadful *faux pas;*
    She loosened a stay
    On her *décolleté*
Thus exposing her *je ne sais quoi.*[8]

"Gracious me," said the Duke of Buckleugh,
"I've been struck from the rolls of *Who's Who!*
    All because I was found
    Lying nude on the ground
With my granny, and very nice, too!"

There was a young harlot named Bunny
Whose kisses were sweeter than honey;
    Her callers galore
    Would line up at her door
To take turns in paying her money.

A naughty old colonel of Butte
Had a habit his friends thought was cutte.
    He'd slip off to Spokane
    And proceed from the train
To a house of distinct ill reputte.

8. Or:

    A girl while attending Bryn Mawr
    Was pinched by her low strapless bra.
        She loosened one wire—
        Whereupon the entire
    Dress fell, and left her quite raw.

Aubrey Beardsley

C: *"There was a young Turkish cadet— . . ."*

There was a young Turkish cadet—
And this is the damnedest one yet—
    His tool was so long
    And incredibly strong
He could bugger six Greeks *en brochette.*

There was a young lady named Cager
Who, as the result of a wager,
    Consented to fart
    The whole oboe part
Of Mozart's *Quartet in F Major.*

There was a young cashier of Calais
Whose accounts, when reviewed, wouldn't talais;
    Soon his chief smelled a rat,
    For he'd furnished a flat,
And was seen every night at the balais.

There was a young man of Calcutta
Who had an unfortunate stutter.
    "I would like," he once said,
    "Some b-b-b-bread
And also some b-b-b-butter."[1]

1. Edward Lear wrote the first "Calcutta-butter" limerick and Ogden Nash wrote a better one. Our own favorite "Calcutta" limerick, however, abandons the rhyme with "butter":

    An unfortunate lad from Calcutta
    Vibrated all through from his stutter;
        To eat, walk or speak
        He would shake for a week
    But he *was* rather good as a rutter.

There once was a monk of Camyre
Who was seized with a carnal desire.
    And the primary cause
    Was the abbess' drawers
Which were hung up to dry by the fire.

There was a young girl of Cape Cod
Who thought babies were fashioned by God,
    But 'twas not the Almighty
    Who hiked up her nightie—
'Twas Roger the lodger, by God!

A menagerie came to Cape Race
Where they loved the gorilla's grimace.
    It surprised them to learn
    That he *owned* the concern:
He was human, in spite of his face!

A hot-tempered girl of Caracas
Was wed to a samba-mad jackass;
    When he started to cheat her
    With a dark senorita
She kicked him right in the maracas.

There was a young fellow named Cass
Whose ballocks were made out of brass.
  When they tinkled together
  They played *Stormy Weather*,
And lightning shot out of his ass.

There was a co-ed of Cayenne
Who ate onions, blue cheese and sen-sen,
  Till a bad fright one day
  Took her breath quite away,
And we hope she won't find it again.

A venturesome three-weeks-old chamois
Strayed off in the woods from his mamois,
  And might have been dead
  But some picknickers fed
Him with sandwiches, milk, and salamois.

A lady with features cherubic
Was famed for her area pubic.
  When they asked her its size
  She replied in surprise,
"Are you speaking of square feet, or cubic?"

A vessel has sailed from Chicago
With barrels of pork for a cargo;
 For Boston she's bound,
 Preceded, I've found,
By another with beans from near Fargo.

There was a young lady of Chichester
Who made all the saints in their niches stir.
 One morning at matins
 Her breasts in white satin
Made the Bishop of Chichester's britches stir.

There was a young man from the city
Who met what he thought was a kitty.
 He gave it a pat
 And said, "Nice little cat."
They buried his clothes, out of pity.

A Salvation lassie named Claire
Was having her first love affair.
 As she climbed into bed
 She reverently said,
"I wish to be opened with prayer."

André Domin

There once was a co-ed named Clapper
In psychology class, quite a napper—
    But her Freudian dreams
    Were so classic, it seems
That now she's a Phi Beta Kappa.[2]

A desperate spinster from Clare
Once knelt in the moonlight all bare.
    And prayed to her God
    For a romp on the sod—
A passer-by answered her prayer.

The bashful young bachelor Cleary
Of girls was exceedingly leary;
    Then a lady named Lou
    Showed him how and with who
He could render his evenings more cheery.

A cabin boy on an old clipper
Grew steadily flipper and flipper.
    He plugged up his ass
    With fragments of glass
And thus circumcised his old skipper.

2. The work of Harvey L. Carter, professor of history
at Colorado College.

There was a young fellow from Clyde
Who once at a funeral was spied.
　　When asked who was dead,
　　He smilingly said,
"I don't know. I just came for the ride."

There was a young harlot of Clyde
Whose doctor cut open her hide.
　　He misplaced his stitches
　　And closed the wrong niches;
She now does her work on the side.

There was a young man from the Coast
Who had an affair with a ghost.
　　At the height of orgasm
　　This she-ectoplasm
Said, "I think I can feel it—almost."

There was a young man of Coblenz
Whose equipment was simply immense.
　　It took forty-four draymen,
　　A priest and three laymen
To carry it thither and thence.

Aubrey Beardsley

A certain old maid in Cohoes
In despair taught her bird to propose;
    But the parrot, dejected
    At being accepted,
Spoke some lines too profane to disclose.

There was a young man of Cohoes
Who diddled himself with his toes.
    He did it so neat
    He betrothed his own feet,
And christened them Myrtle and Rose.

An unpopular youth of Cologne
With a pain in his stomach did mogne.
    He heaved a great sigh,
    And said, "I would digh,
But the loss would be only my ogne."

There was a young man named Colquhoun
Who kept as a pet a babuhoun.
    His mother said, "Cholmondeley,
    I don't think it's quite colmondeley
To feed your babuhoun with spuhoun."

There was a young lady of Condover
Whose husband had ceased to be fond of her.
    He could not forget
    He had wooed a brunette
But peroxide had now made a blonde of her.

A very smart lady named Cookie
Said, "I like to mix gambling with nookie.
    Before every race
    I go home to my place
And curl up with a very good bookie."

A senora who strolled on the Corso
Displayed quite a lot of her torso.
    A crowd soon collected
    And no one objected
Though some were in favor of more so.

A certain young gourmet of Crediton
Took some pâté de foie gras and spread it on
    A chocolate biscuit
    Then murmured, "I'll risk it":
His tomb bears the date that he said it on.[3]

3. Written by the Reverend Charles Inge.

A lady while dining at Crewe
Found an elephant's whang in her stew.
　　Said the waiter, "Don't shout,
　　Or wave it about,
Or the others will all want one too."[4]

There was an old fellow from Croydon,
Whose cook was a cute little hoyden.
　　She would sit on his knees
　　While shelling the peas
Or pleasanter duties employed on.

A fanatic gun-lover named Crust
Was perverse to the point of disgust:
　　His idea of a peach
　　Had a sixteen-inch breech
And a pearl-handled .44 bust.

There once was a young man named Cyril
Who was had in a wood by a squirrel,
　　And he liked it so good
　　That he stayed in the wood
Just as long as the squirrel stayed virile.

4. One of many famous "Crewe" limericks. Others:

A railroad official at Crewe
Met an engine one day that he knew.
　　Though he nodded and bowed
　　The engine was proud,
And it cut him—it cut him in two.

A society climber from Crewe
Inquired, "What on earth shall I do?
　　I of course know what's that
　　But I fear I have not
The faintest idea of who's who."

There was a young lady of Crewe
Who wanted to catch the 2:02.
　　Said a porter, "Don't worry,
　　Or hurry, or scurry,
It's a minute or two to 2:02."

D: *"A team playing baseball in Dallas . . ."*

A team playing baseball in Dallas
Called the umpire names out of malice.
    While that worthy had fits,
    The team made eight hits
And a girl in the bleachers named Alice.

A book and a jug and a dame,
And a nice cozy nook for the same;
    "And I don't care a damn,"
    Said Omar Khayyam,
"What you say, it's a great little game."

There was a young girl of Darjeeling
Who could dance with such exquisite feeling
    Not a murmur was heard,
    Not a sound, not a word,
But the fly-buttons hitting the ceiling.

An assistant professor named Ddodd
Had manners arresting and odd.
    He said, "If you please,
    Spell my name with four 'd's."
Though one was sufficient for God.

"Well, Madam," the Bishop declared,
While the Vicar just mumbled and stared,
    " 'Twere better, perhaps,
    In the crypt or the apse,
Because sex in the nave must be shared."

There was a young lady of Dee
Went to bed with each man she would see.
    When it came to a test
    She wished to be best,
And practice makes perfect, you see.[1]

Well bugged was a boy named Delpasse
By all of the lads in his class.
    He said, with a yawn,
    "Now the novelty's gone
It's only a pain in the ass."

There was a young girl of Detroit
Who at fucking was very adroit;
    She could shrink her vagina
    To a pin-point or fina
And then toss it out like a quoit.[2]

1. Or:

There was a young lady named Flo
Whose lover was almighty slow.
    So they tried it all night
    Till he got it just right,
For practice makes pregnant, you know.

2. There is a sequel:

She married a man from the Strand
Who had a most unusual stand.
    He would take on a midge
    Or the arch of a bridge:
To see them together was grand.

"I must leave here," said Lady de Vere,
"For these damp airs don't suit me, I fear."
    Said her friend, "Goodness me!
    If they do not agree
With your system, why eat pears, my dear?"

There was a young man of Devizes
Whose testes were two different sizes.
    The one was so small
    It was no ball at all;
But the other one won several prizes.

There was a young lady of Devon
Who was raped in the garden by seven
    High Anglican priests—
    The lascivious beasts—
Of such is the Kingdom of Heaven.

The eminent Mme. DeVue
Was born in a cage at the zoo,
    And the curious rape
    Which made her an ape
Is highly fantastic, if true.

There was a young fellow named Dice
Who remarked, "They say bigamy's nice.
    Even two are a bore,
    I'd prefer three or four,
For the plural of spouse, it is spice."

When the Bishop of Solomons diocese
Was stricken with elephantiasis,
    The public beheld
    His balls as they swelled
By paying exorbitant priocese.

A complacent old Don of Divinity
Made boast of his daughter's virginity.
    They must have been dawdlin'
    Down at old Magdalen—
It couldn't have happened at Trinity.

"I wouldn't be bothered with drawers,"
Says one of our better-known whawers;
    "There isn't much doubt
    I do better without
In handling my everyday chawers."

Aubrey Beardsley

A young Irish servant in Drogheda
Had a mistress who often annogheda,
    Whereupon she would swear
    In a language so rare
That thereafter nobody emplogheda.

A surly and pessimist Druid,
A defeatist, if only he knew it,
    Said, "The world's on the skids
    And I think having kids
Is a waste of good seminal fluid."

The grandniece of Madame DuBarry
Suspected her son was a fairy;
    "It's peculiar," said she,
    "But he sits down to pee,
And he stands when I bathe the canary."

Once out on the lake at Dubuque,
A girl took a sail with a duque.
    He remarked, "I am sure
    You are honest and pure"—
And then leaned far over to puque.

A dentist who lives in Duluth
Has wedded a widow named Ruth.
   ·She is so sentimental
    Concerning things dental
She calls her dear second her twoth.

There was a young man of Dumfries
Who said to his girl, "If you please,
    It would give me great bliss
    If, while playing with this,
You would pay some attention to these."

There was a young man from Dunbar
Who playfully pickled his ma.
    When he finished his work
    He remarked with a smirk,
"This will make quite a family jar."

A rosy-cheeked lass from Dunellen
Whom the Hoboken sailors call Helen
    In her efforts to please
    Has spread social disease
From New York to the Straits of Magellan.

André Domin

A bibulous chap from Duquesne
Drank a whole jeraboam of champuesne.
    Said he with a laugh,
    As he quaffed the last quaff,
"I tried to get drunk, but in vuesne."

Let us now broach a firkin to Durkin,
Addicted to jerkin' his gherkin;
    His wife said, "Now, Durkin,
    By jerkin' your gherkin
You're shirkin' your firkin'—you bastard."

To his wife said a grumbler named Dutton,
"I'm a gourmet, I am, not a glutton.
    For ham, jam, or lamb
    I don't give a damn.
Come on, let's return to our mutton."

E: *"There was a young man of Eau Claire . . ."*

There was a young man of Eau Claire,
Enjoying his girl on the stair;
    On the forty-fourth stroke,
    The banister broke
And he finished her off in mid-air.

There was an old fellow of Eire
Who perpetually sat on the fire.
    When they asked, "Are you hot?"
    He declared, "I am not.
I am Pat Winterbottom, Esquire."

The new cinematic emporium
Is not just a super-sensorium,
    But a highly effectual
    Heterosexual
Mutual masturbatorium.

There was a young lady named Erskine
Who had a remarkably fair skin;
    When I said to her, "Mabel,
    You'd look nice in sable,"
She replied, "I look best in my bare skin."

An unfortunate maiden named Esther,
A peculiar repugnance possessed her:
    A reaction compulsive
    Made kissing repulsive,
Which was rough on all those who caressed her.

There was a young lady of Eton,
Whose figure had plenty of meat on.
    She said, "Marry me, dear,
    And you'll find that my rear
Is a nice place to warm your cold feet on."

There was a young lady named Etta
Who fancied herself in a sweater;
    Three reasons she had:
    To keep warm was not bad,
But the other two reasons were better.

There was a young lady named Eva
Who filled up her bath to receiva.
    She took off her clothes
    From her head to her toes,
And a voice from the keyhole yelled, "Beava!"

André Domin

There was a young lady of Exeter,
So pretty the men craned their necks at her;
    And one was so brave
    As to take out and wave
The distinguishing mark of his sex at her.

 F: *"In Summer he said she was fair . . ."*

In Summer he said she was fair,
In Autumn her charms were still there;
    But he said to his wife
    In the Winter of life,
"There's no Spring in your old *derrière*."

A strip-teaser up in Fall River
Caused a sensitive fellow to quiver.
    The esthetic vibration
    Brought soulful elation:
Besides, it was good for the liver.

A wartime young lady of fashion,
Much noted for wit and for passion,
    Is known to have said
    As she jumped into bed,
"Here's one thing those bastards can't ration."

There was an old spinster from Fife
Who had never been kissed in her life;
    Along came a cat
    And she said, "I'll kiss that!"
But the cat meowed, "Not on your life!"

There was a young fellow named Fisher
Who was fishing for fish in a fissure;
    Then a cod with a grin
    Pulled the fisherman in . . .
Now they're fishing the fissure for Fisher.

A newspaper writer named Fling
Could make copy from most anything;
    But the copy he wrote
    Of a ten-dollar note
Was so good he is now in Sing Sing.

There was a young lady of Florence
Who for kissing professed great abhorrence;
    But when she'd been kissed
    And found what she'd missed,
She cried till the tears came in torrents.

Concerning the bees and the flowers
In the fields and the gardens and bowers,
    You will note at a glance
    That their ways of romance
Haven't any resemblance to ours.

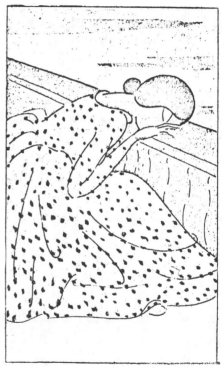

André Domin

Aubrey Beardsley

A reckless young man from Fort Blainy
Made love to a spinster named Janie.
    When his friends said, "Oh, dear,
    She's so old and so queer,"
He replied, "But the day was *so* rainy!"

On her bosom a beauteous young frail
Had illumined the price of her tail;
    And on her behind,
    For the sake of the blind,
The same is embroidered in Braille.

A publisher once went to France
In search of a tale of romance;
    A Parisian lady
    Told a story so shady
That the publisher made an advance.

"My dear, you've been kissing young Fred,"
A much-worried mother once said,
    "Since six; it's now ten;
    Do it just once again,
And then think of going to bed."

There was a young artist named Frentzel
Whose tool was as sharp as a pencil.
    He pricked through an actress,
    The sheet and the mattress,
And punctured the bedroom utensil.

Ah, Vienna, the fortress of Freud!
Whose surgeons are always employed;
    Where boys with soft hands
    Are provided with glands,
And two-fisted girls are de-boyed.

I once thought a lot of a friend
Who turned out to be in the end
    The southernmost part
    (As I'd feared from the start)
Of a horse with a northerly trend.

There was a young girl whose frigidity
Approached cataleptic rigidity
    Till you gave her a drink
    When she quickly would sink
In a state of complaisant liquidity.

André Domin

Take the case of a lady named Frost
Whose organ is three feet across.
    It's the best part of valor
    To bugger the gal or
One's apt to fall in and get lost.

 G: *"A lady from way down in Ga. . . ."*

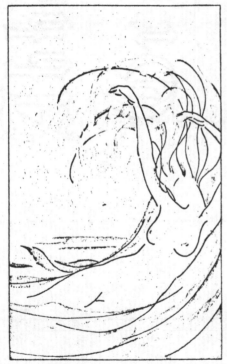

André Domin

A lady from way down in Ga.
Became quite a notable fa.
    But she faded from view
    With a quaint I. O. U.
That she signed, "Miss Lucrezia Ba."

There once lived a certain Miss Gale,
Who turned most exceedingly pale,
    For a mouse climbed her leg
    (Don't repeat this, I beg)
And a splinter got caught in its tail.

There once were three fellows from Gary
Named Larry and Harry and Barry;
    Now Harry was bare
    As an egg or a pear,
But Larry and Barry were hairy.

There was a young lady named Gay
Who was asked to make love in the hay;
    She jumped at the chance
    And took off her pants:
She was tickled to try it that way.

A homely young harlot named Gert
Used to streetwalk until her corns hurt;
　　But now she just stands
　　Upside down on her hands
With her face covered up by her skirt.

There once was a young man of Ghent
Whose tool was so long that it bent.
　　To save himself trouble
　　He put it in double,
And instead of coming, he went.

A fellow with passions quite gingery
Was exploring his young sister's lingerie;
　　Then with giggles of pleasure
　　He plundered her treasure—
Adding incest to insult and injury.

There was a young woman of Glasgow
Whose party proved quite a fiasco;
　　At nine-thirty, about,
　　The lights all went out
Through a lapse on the part of the gas co.

André Domin

André Domin

A neurotic young playboy named Gleason
Liked boys for no tangible reason.
    A frontal lobotomy
    Cured him of sodomy
But ruined his plans for the season.

There was a young lady named Gloria
Who'd been had by Sir Gerald Du Maurier,
    And then by six men,
    Sir Gerald again,
And the band at the Waldorf-Astoria.

There was a young girl from old Gloucester
Whose parents were sure they had lost her,
    Till they came in the grass
    To the marks of her ass
And the knees of the man who had crossed her.

In Paris some visitors go
To see what no person should know.
    And then there are tourists,
    The purest of purists,
Who say it is quite *comme il faut*.

There was a young peasant named Gorse
Who fell madly in love with his horse.
    Said his wife, "You rapscallion
    That horse is a stallion—
This constitutes grounds for divorce."

A God-fearing maiden from Goshen
Took a September-morn swim in the ocean;
    When a whirlpool appeared
    She rose up and cheered
And developed a rotary motion.

There was a young lady named Grace
Who had eyes in a very odd place.
    She could sit on the hole
    Of a mouse or a mole
And stare the beast square in the face.

There once was a maid with such graces
That her curves cried aloud for embraces.
    "You look," cried each he,
    "Like a million to me—
Invested in *all* the right places!"

André Domin

A painter who came from Great Britain
Hailed a lady who sat with her knitain.
 He remarked with a sigh,
 "That park bench—well, I
Just painted it, right where you're sitain."

Winter is here with his grouch;
The time when you sneeze and you slouch;
 You can't take your women
 Canoeing or swimming—
But a lot can be done on a couch!

A daring young lady of Guam
Observed, "The Pacific's so calm
 I'll swim out for a lark."
 She met a large shark . . .
Let us now sing the Ninetieth Psalm.

Have you heard of the knock-kneed Sam Guzzum,
And Samantha, his bow-legged cousin?
 There are some people say
 That love finds a way,
But for Sam and Samantha it doesn't.

H: *"A mathematician named Hall . . ."*

A mathematician named Hall
Has a hexahedronical ball,
    And the cube of its weight
    Times his pecker, plus eight,
Is his phone number—give him a call.

A modern young lady named Hall
Attended a birth-control ball.
    She was loaded with pessaries
    And other accessories—
But no one approached her at all.

A prolific young mother named Hall
Who seemed to have triplets each Fall,
    When asked why and wherefore,
    Said, "That's what we're here for,
But we often get nothing at all."

There was a young fellow named Hall
Who confessed, "I have only one ball,
    But the size of my prick
    Is God's dirtiest trick;
For the girls always ask, 'Is that all?' "

There was a young fellow named Hammer
Who had an unfortunate stammer.
    "The b-bane of my life,"
    Said he, "is m-my wife."
D–d–d–d–d–d–damn 'er!"

It always delights me at Hanks
To walk up the old river banks.
    One time in the grass
    I stepped on an ass
And heard a young girl murmur, "Thanks!"

A certain young lady named Hannah
Was caught in a flood in Montannah.
    As she floated away
    Her beau, so they say,
Accompanied her on the piannah.

There was a sweet lassie named Harriet
Who would take on two lads in a chariot,
    Then six monks and four tailors,
    Nine priests and eight sailors,
Mohammed and Judas Iscariot.

Aubrey Beardsley

André Domin

There once was a lady named Harris
That nothing seemed apt to embarrass
    Till the bathsalts she shook
    In a tub that she took
Turned out to be plaster–of–Paris.

There was an old lady of Harrow
Whose views were exceedingly narrow.
    At the end of her paths
    She built two bird baths
For the different sexes of sparrow.

There was a young lady of Harwich
Who behaved very bad at her marich:
    She proceeded on skates
    To the parish church gates,
While her friends followed on in a carwich.

A baritone star of Havana
Slipped horribly on a banana;
    He was sick for a year
    Then resumed his career
As a promising lyric soprano.

A flatulent nun of Hawaii
One Easter eve supped on papaya,
    Then honored the Passover
    By turning her ass over
And obliging with Handel's Messiah.

There was an old man in a hearse,
Who murmured, "This might have been worse;
    Of course the expense
    Is simply immense,
But it doesn't come out of *my* purse."

There was a young girl named Ann Heuser
Who swore that no man could surprise her.
    But Pabst took a chance,
    Found a Schlitz in her pants,
And now she is sadder Budweiser.[1]

There was a young lady named Hilda
Who went driving one night with a builda.
    He said that he should,
    That he could and he would,
And he did and it pretty near killda.

[1]. This classic American example, a great favorite in St. Louis, might be called a draft for a limerick.

André Domin

"It's no good," said Lady Maud Hoare,
"I can't concentrate any more.
    You're all in a sweat
    And the sheets are quite wet,
And just look at the time—half past four."

There was a young man of Hong Kong
Who invented a topical song.
    It wasn't the words
    That bothered the birds,
But the horrible *double ontong*.

There was a young maiden named Hoople
Whose bosom was triple, not douple;
    So she had one removed
    But it grew back improved
And at present her front is quadruple.

A hapless church tenor was Horace
Whose skin was so terribly porous,
    Sometimes in the choir
    He'd start to perspire,
And nearly drown out the whole chorus.

There once was a fellow named Howells
Had a terrible time with his bowels.
    His wife, so they say,
    Cleaned them out every day
With special elongated trowels.

There was a young fellow named Hyde
Who fell down a privy and died.
    His unfortunate brother
    Then fell down another,
And now they're interred side by side.[2]

2. Somewhat off-color—and the only such limerick that Langdon Reed ever allowed to appear in any of his many books. It's to be feared that Reed did not get the pun in the last line.

I: *"The Bishop of Ibu Plantation . . ."*

The Bishop of Ibu Plantation
Wrote a thesis on Transfiguration
    For *The Christian Review*
    (As all good Bishops do)
While practicing miscegenation.

The Kings of Peru were the Incas,
Who were known far and wide as great drincas.
    They worshipped the sun
    And had lots of fun,
But the peons all thought them great stincas.

Our Vicar is good Mr. Inge.
One evening he offered to sing.
    So we asked him to stoop,
    Put his head in a loop,
And pulled at each end of the string.

In Wall Street a girl named Irene
Made an offering somewhat obscene:
    She stripped herself bare
    And offered a share
To Merrill Lynch, Pierce, Fenner and Beane.[1]

[1] A fine limerick ruined by a change of name: the company is now Merrill Lynch, Pierce, Fenner and Smith.

J: *"There was a young person of Jaipur . . ."*

There was a young person of Jaipur
Who fell madly in love with a viper.
    With screams of delight
    He'd retire each night
With the viper concealed in his diaper.

An impish young fellow named James
Had a passion for idiot games.
    He lighted the hair
    Of his lady's affair,
And laughed as she peed out the flames.

There was a great lord in Japan
Whose name on a Tuesday began;
    It carried through Sunday
    Till twilight on Monday,
And sounded like stones in a can.

There once was a young girl named Jeanie
Whose Dad was a terrible meanie:
    He fashioned a latch
    And a hatch for her snatch—
She could only be had by Houdini.

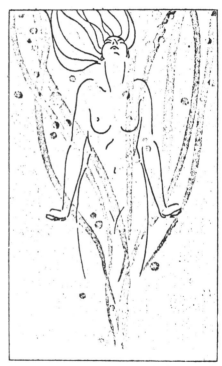

André Domin

Nymphomaniacal Jill
Tried a dynamite stick for a thrill;
    They found her vagina
    In North Carolina
And bits of her tits in Brazil.

There once was a damsel named Jinx,
Who when asked what she thought of the Sphinx,
    Replied with a smile,
    "That old fraud by the Nile?
I personally think that she stinks."

There was a young student named Jones
Who'd reduce any maiden to moans
    By his wonderful knowledge,
    Acquired in college,
Of nineteen erogenous zones.

There was a young maiden of Joppa
Who came a society cropper.
    She went off to Ostend
    With a gentleman friend,
And the rest of the story's improper.[1]

1. Attributed to the late Samuel Hopkins Adams.

 K: *"There's a lady in Kalamazoo . . ."*

There's a lady in Kalamazoo
Who first bites her oysters in two;
    She has a misgiving
    Should any be living,
They'd raise such a hullabaloo.

There was a young lady named Kate
Who necked in the dark with her date.
    When asked how she fared,
    She said she was scared,
But otherwise doing first-rate.

An impetuous couple named Kelly
Now go through life belly-to-belly
    Because in their haste
    They used library paste
Instead of petroleum jelly.[1]

There was a young lady of Kent
Who said that she knew what it meant
    When men asked her to dine,
    Gave her cocktails and wine:
She knew what it meant, but she went.

1. Legend has it that this limerick was told as the beginning of a speech to an American literary association by a visiting English writer of great celebrity. His audience, we regret to say, walked out on him.

There was a young harlot from Kew
Who filled her vagina with glue.
    She said with a grin,
    "If they pay to get in,
They'll pay to get out of it, too."

A pansy who lived in Khartoum
Took a lesbian up to his room,
    And they argued a lot
    About who would do what
And how and with which and to whom.

There was an old girl ot Kilkenny,
Whose usual charge was a penny.
    For half of that sum
    You might fondle her bum:
A source of amusement to many.

There was a young fellow named Kimble
Whose prick was exceedingly nimble
    But so fragile and slender
    And dainty and tender
He kept it encased in a thimble.

André Domin

André Domin

Said a fair-headed maiden of Klondike,
"Of you I'm exceedingly fond, Ike.
    To prove I adore you
    I'll dye, darling, for you,
And be a brunette, not a blonde, Ike."

A corpulent lady named Kroll
Had an idea exceedingly droll:
    She went to a ball
    Dressed in nothing at all
And backed in as a Parker House roll.

 L: *"There was a young fellow named Lancelot . . ."*

There was a young fellow named Lancelot
Whom his neighbors all looked on askance a lot.
    Whenever he'd pass
    A presentable lass
The front of his pants would advance a lot.

There was a young girl of La Plata
Who was widely renowned as a farta.
    Her deafening reports
    At the Argentine sports
Made her much in demand as a starta.

In the garden remarked Lord Larkeeding:
"A fig for your digging and weeding.
    I like watching birds
    While they're dropping their turds,
And spying on guinea pigs breeding."

Roasalina, a pretty young lass
Had a truly magnificent ass:
    Not rounded and pink,
    As you possibly think—
It was gray, had long ears, and ate grass.

A rascal far gone in lechery
Lured maids to their doom by his treachery.
    He invited them in
    For the purpose of sin,
Though he said 'twas to look at his etchery.

A doughty old person in Leeds
Rashly swallowed a package of seeds.
    In a month his poor ass
    Was all covered with grass
And he couldn't sit down for the weeds.

A renegade priest from Liberia
Whose morals were clearly inferior
    Once did to a nun
    What he shouldn't have done,
And now she's a Mother Superior.

There once was a lady named Lilly
With a craving to walk Piccadilly:
    Said she, "Ain't it funny,
    It's not for the money,
But if I don't take it, it's silly!"

André Domin

André Domin

An effeminate fellow from Lincoln
One night did some serious drincoln,
    Met a gal, now his wife,
    Learned the true facts of life,
And blesses the day he got stincoln.

A visitor once to Loch Ness
Met the monster, who left him a mess;
    They returned his entrails
    By the regular mails
And the rest of the stuff by express.

There's a singer in Long Island City
Whose form is impressively pretty;
    She is often addressed
    By the name of "Beau Chest,"
Which is thought to be tasteful and witty.

The team of Tom and Louise
Do an act in the nude on their knees.
    They crawl down the aisle
    While screwing dog-style
And the orchestra plays Kilmer's "Trees."

There was a young lady of Louth
Who returned from a trip to the South.
    Her father said, "Nelly,
    There's more in your belly
Than ever went in by your mouth."[1]

A plumber from Lowater Creek
Was called in by a dame with a leak;
    She looked so becoming
    He fixed *all* her plumbing,
And didn't emerge for a week.

An eccentric old spinster named Lowell
Announced to her friends, "Bless my sowell,
    I've gained so much weight
    I am sorry to state
I fear that I'm going to fowell."

Have you heard about Magda Lupescu,
Who came to Rumania's rescue?
    It's a wonderful thing
    To be under a king—
Is democracy better, I esk you?[2]

1. Norman Douglas said of this limerick: "The words uttered by the father will suffice to date this poem: it belongs to the Victorian era." He called it "an elegant example of the Golden Period."

2. One of the best and most presentable of the one-time "topical" limericks. Dozens of others—concerning such notables as Mary Astor and Brenda Diana Duff-Frazier—were reviewed for this book and found unsuitable.

3. For some reason this limerick by Harlan Logan failed to win the Salada Tea contest to which he submitted it. Mike Nichols, once asked to judge a limerick contest, is reported to have said: "It was easy. We just threw out the dirty limericks and gave the prize to the one that was left." The Young Lady from Lynn is the heroine of many other limericks, of which two of the best are:

> There was a young lady of Lynn
> Who was deep in original sin;
> >   When they said, "Do be good!"
> >   She said, "Would if I could!"
> And straightway went at it again.

> There was a young lady of Lynn
> Who thought all love-making a sin;
> >   But when she got tight
> >   It seemed quite all right,
> So everyone plied her with gin.

A whole sequence concerns the Young Lady from Lynn "who was so uncommonly thin":

> There was a young lady of Lynn
> Who was nothing but bones except skin;
> >   So she wore a false bust
> >   In the likewise false trust
> That she looked like a lady of sin.

There was a young lady from Lynn
Who could pee on the head of a pin
>   By filling her bladder
>   With a quart of Salada
And letting it out very thin![3]

 M: *"An amorous M. A. . . ."*

An amorous M. A.
Said of Cupid, the C. D.,
 "From their prodigal use,
 He is, I deduce,
The John Jacob A. H."

There once was a lady named Mabel
So ready, so willing, so able,
 And so full of spice
 She could name her own price—
Now Mabel's all wrapped up in sable.[1]

There was a young girl from Madrid
Who learned she was having a kid.
 By holding her water
 Two months and a quarter,
She drowned the poor bastard, she did.

There was a young lady of Maine
Who declared she'd a man on the brain.
 But you knew from the view
 Of her waist as it grew
It was not on her brain that he'd lain.[2]

1. Or:

There was a young lady named Mabel
Who said, "I don't think that I'm able;
 But I'm willing to try
 So where shall I lie—
On the bed, on the floor or the table?"

2. Or:

There was a young fellow in Maine
Who courted a girl all in vain;
 She cussed when he kissed her
 So he slept with her sister
Again and *again* and AGAIN.

There once was maitre d'hotel
Who said, "They can all go to hell!
     What they do to my wife
     Is the ruin of my life,
And the worst is, they do it so well."

There was a young girl who would make
Advances to snake after snake.
     She said, "I'm not vicious,
     But so superstitious!
I do it for grandmother's sake."

To Sadie the touch of a male meant
An emotional cardiac ailment;
     And acuteness of breath
     Caused her untimely death
In the course of erotic impalement.

A dentist, young Doctor Malone,
Got a charming girl patient alone,
     And, in his depravity,
     He filled the wrong cavity—
Just see how his practice has grown!

André Domin

There was a young lady of Malta
Who strangled her aunt with a halter.
    She said, "I won't bury her;
    She'll do for my terrier.
She should keep for a month if I salt her."

If Leo your own birthday marks
You will lust until forty, when starts
    A new pleasure in stamps,
    Boy Scouts and their camps,
And fondling nude statues in parks.

There was a young lady named Maude,
A sort of society fraud.
    In the parlor, 'tis told,
    She was distant, and cold,
But on the verandah, my Gawd![3]

There once was an African Mau-Mau
Who got into a rather bad row-row.
    The cause of the friction
    Was his practicing diction,
Saying, "How–how now–now brown–brown cow–
        cow."

3. A famous old limerick, enshrined by Bennett Cerf as one of his all-time "Big Ten."

There was a young farmer named Max
Who avoided the gasoline tax;
　　It was simple, you see,
　　For his Vespa burned pee
From his grandfather's herd of tame yaks.

On a picnic a Scot named McFee
Was stung in the balls by a bee.
　　He made oodles of money
　　By oozing pure honey
Each time he attempted to pee.

A disgusting young man named McGill
Made his neighbors exceedingly ill
　　When they learned of his habits
　　Involving white rabbits
And a bird with a flexible bill.

The cross-eyed old painter McNeff
Was color-blind, palsied, and deaf;
　　When he asked to be touted
　　The critics all shouted:
"This is art, with a capital F!"

André Domin

André Domin

There was an old Scot named McTavish
Who attempted an anthropoid ravish.
 The object of rape
  Was the wrong sex of ape,
And the anthropoid ravished McTavish.

A lady who came from Mobile
Had parts made of Bessemer steel.
 She could only get thrills
  From mechanical drills
Or an off-center emery wheel.

A dentist named Archibald Moss
Fell in love with the dainty Miss Ross,
 But he held in abhorrence
  Her Christian name, Florence,
So he renamed her his Dental Floss.

A lady on climbing Mount Shasta
Complained as the mountain grew vaster,
 That it wasn't the climb
  Nor the dirt nor the grime
But the ice on her ass that harassed her.

She frowned and called him Mr.
Because in sport he kr.
    And so in spite
    That very night
This Mr. kr. sr.

A gentle old dame they called Muir
Had a mind so delightfully pure
    That she fainted away
    At a friend's house one day
When she saw some canary manure.

There was a young maiden from Multerry,
Whose knowledge of life was desultory;
    She explained, like a sage,
    "Adolescence? The stage
Between puberty and—er—adultery."

Astute Melanesians on Munda
Heard a padre discussing the wunda
    Of Virginal Birth;
    They debated its worth,
Then tore the poor padre asunda.

André Domin

There was a young eunuch from Munich
Who wore a lascivious tunic.
    It was woven with care
    Out of fine pubic hair
In patterns both rubric and runic.

There was a young lady from Munich
Who had an affair with a eunuch.
    At the height of their passion
    He dealt her a ration
From a squirt gun concealed in his tunic.

A remarkable feature has Myrtle,
A retractable tail like a turtle;
    But though she has never
    Been called cute or clever
She annually proves to be fertile.

 N: *"There was a young man from Natal . . ."*

André Domin

There was a young man from Natal
And Sue was the name of his gal.
    He went out one day
    For a rather long way—
In fact, right up Sue'z Canal.

The tax-paying whores of the nation
Sent Congress a large delegation
    To convince those old fools
    Their professional tools
Were subject to depreciation.

A young girl of English nativity
Had a fanny of rare sensitivity.
    She could sit on the lap
    Of a Nazi or Jap
And detect his Fifth Column activity.

There was a young girl of Navarre
Who was frightfully fond of a tar.
    When she followed him over
    From Calais to Dover,
Her friends cried, "That's going too far!"

He hated to sew, so young Ned
Rang the bell of his neighbor instead;
  But her husband said, "Vi,
  When you stitched his torn fly,
There was *no* need to bite off the thread."

Brigham Young was never a neutah,
A pansy or fairy or fruitah.
  Where ten thousand virgins
  Succumbed to his urgin's
We now have the great state of Utah.

There was a young girl of New York
Who plugged up her privates with cork.
  A woodpecker or two
  Made the grade, it is true,
But it totally baffled the stork.

When you think of the hosts without no.
Who are slain by the deadly cuco.
  It's quite a mistake
  Of such food to partake:
It results in a permanent slo.

A bobby from Nottingham Junction,
Whose organ had long ceased to function,
    Deceived his good wife
    For the rest of her life
With the aid of his constable's truncheon.

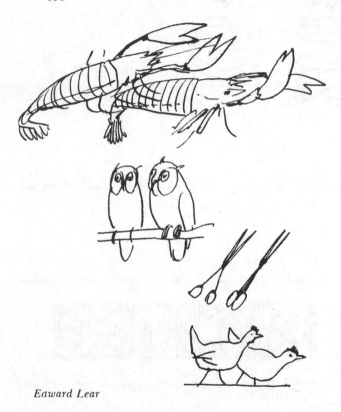

Edward Lear

 O: *"A hermit once thought his oasis . . ."*

Aubrey Beardsley

A hermit once thought his oasis
The best of all possible places;
    For it had a mirage
    In the form of a large
And affectionate female curvaceous.

There was a young girl of Odessa
A rather unblushing transgressor;
    When sent to the priest
    The lewd little beast
Began to undress her confessor.

Have you heard of the Widow O'Reilly,
Who esteemed her late husband so highly
    That in spite of the scandal
    Her umbrella handle
Was made of his *membrum virile?*

There was a young maid of Ostend
Who swore she'd hold out to the end;
    But, alas, halfway over
    From Calais to Dover
She done what she didn't intend.

P: *"Said a charming young lady of Padua . . ."*

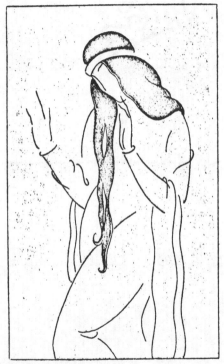

André Domin

Said a charming young lady of Padua,
"A peso! Why, sir, what a cadua!"
    He said, lifting his hat,
    "You ain't even worth that.
However, I'm glad to have hadua."

An alluring young shoat of Paree
Fills all of her suitors with glee,
    For when they implore
    Her to give a bit more,
She invariably answers, "Wee, wee."

There was a young warrior of Parma
Who got into bed with his charma.
    She, naturally nude,
    Said, "Don't think me rude,
But I *do* wish you'd take off your arma!"

There was a young lady of Pecking
Who indulged in a great deal of necking;
    This seemed a great waste
    Since she claimed to be chaste;
This statement, however, needs checking.

There was a young girl of Penzance
Who decided to take just one chance.
    So she let herself go
    In the arms of her beau;
Now all of her sisters are aunts.

On May Day the girls of Penzance
Being bored by a lack of romance,
    Joined the workers' parade
    With this banner displayed:
"What the Pants of Penzance Need Is Ants."

There was an old Justice named Percival,
Who said, "I suppose you'll get worse if I'll
    Send you to jail,
    So I'll put you on bail."
Now wasn't Judge Percival merciful?

The Shah of the Empire of Persia
Lay for days in a sexual merger.
    When the nautch asked the Shah,
    "Won't you ever withdraw?"
He replied, "It's not love; it's inertia."[1]

1. A remarkable race are the Persians:
    They have such peculiar diversions.
      They make love all day
      In the regular way,
    And save up the nights for perversions.

There was a young fellow named Pete
Who was gentle, and shy, and discreet;
 But with his first woman
 He became quite inhuman
And constantly roared for fresh meat.[2]

They've buried a salesman named Phipps.
He married on one of his trips
 A widow named Block
 Then died of the shock
When he found there were five little chips.

Despite her impressive physique
Fatima was really quite meek;
 If a mouse showed its head
 She would jump into bed
With a terrible blood-curdling sheik.

The girls who frequent picture-palaces
Set no store by psychoanalysis.
 Indeed, they're annoyed
 By the great Dr. Freud
And they cling to their long-standing phalluses.[3]

2. That, of course, was long before the tragic sequel:

There was a young fellow named Pete
Liked to dance in the snow and the sleet.
 One chilly November
 He froze every member
And retired to monkish retreat.

3. In the polite version, *fallacies*. Say it how you will.

An unfortunate lady named Piles
Had the ugliest bottom for miles;
    But her surgeon took pity
    And made it quite pretty:
All dimples, and poutings, and smiles.

There once was a sailor named Pink
Whose mates rushed him off to the clink.
    Said he, "I've a skunk
    As a pet in my bunk—
That's no reason for raising a stink."

There was an old maid of Pitlochry
Whose morals were truly a mockery,
    For under the bed
    Was a lover instead
Of the usual porcelain crockery.

A professor who hailed from Podunk
And was rather too frequently drunk,
    Said, "Sometimes I think
    That I can parse pink:
Let me see—it is pink, pank, and punk."

André Domin

André Domin

An adventurous fun-loving polyp
Propositioned a cute little scallop
    Down under the sea;
    "Nothing doing," said she;
"By Triton—you think I'm a trollop?"

There was a young man from Poughkeepsie
Inclined now and then to get tipsy.
    When afflicted that way
    It was said he would lay
Anything from a sow to a gypsy.

As he filled up his order book pp.
He decided, "I want higher ww."
    So he struck for more pay
    But, alas, now they say
He is sweeping out elephants' cc.

She wasn't what one would call pretty,
And other girls offered her pity;
    So nobody guessed
    That her Wasserman test
Involved half the men in the city.

That elegant gigolo, Price,
Remarked, "Now, it *may* be a vice,
    But one thing I know,
    This dancing for dough
Is something exceedingly nice."

There was a young fellow named Price
Who dabbled in all sorts of vice:
    He had virgins and boys
    And mechanical toys—
And on Mondays, he meddled with mice!

Of a sudden the great prima donna
Cried, "Gawd, but my voice is a goner!"
    But a cat in the wings
    Said, "I know how she sings,"
And finished the solo with honor.

This shortage of help has produced
More kitchen-wise males than it used,
    Like that man of gal*lan*try
    Who, leaving the pantry,
Remarked, "Well, *my* cook is well goosed!"

R: *"There was a young man from Racine . . ."*

There was a young man from Racine
Who invented a fucking machine:
    Both concave and convex,
    It would fit either sex,
With attachments for those in between.[1]

A widow who lived in Rangoon
Hung a black-ribboned wreath on her womb.
    "To remind me," she said,
    "Of my husband, who's dead,
And of what put him into his tomb."

A comely young widow named Ransom
Was ravished three times in a hansom.
    When she cried out for more
    A voice from the floor
Said, "Lady, I'm Simpson, not Samson."

A handsome young bastard named Ray
Was conceived on the Rue de la Paix.
    According to law,
    He can name you his ma,
But as for his pa, *je ne sais*.[2]

1. There are numerous other tag-lines:

And was perfectly simple to clean.

The goddamnedest thing ever seen.

With a saucer beneath for the cream. Etc.

2. Credited to John F. Moore by Louis Untermeyer.

There once was a boring young Rev.
Who preached ill it seemed he would nev.
    His hearers, *en masse,*
    Got a pain in the ass
And prayed for relief of their neth.

There once was a girl from Revere
So enormously large that, oh, dear!
    Once far out in the ocean
    Byrd raised a commotion
By planting our flag on her rear.

An ignorant maiden named Rewdid
Did something amazingly stupid:
    When her lover had spent
    She douched with cement
And gave birth to a statue of Cupid.

There was a young lawyer named Rex
Who was sadly deficient in sex.
    Arraigned for exposure
    He said with composure,
"De minimis non curat lex."[3]

3. "The law is not concerned with trifles."

A glutton who came from the Rhine
Was asked at what hour he'd dine.
    He replied, "At eleven,
    At three, five, and seven,
And eight and a quarter to nine."

A prosperous merchant of Rhone
Fills sexual orders by phone,
    Or the same can be baled,
    Stamped, labeled, and mailed
To a limited parcel-post zone.

A young violinist in Rio
Was seducing a lady named Cleo.
    As she took down her panties,
    She said, "No *andantes;*
I want this *allegro con brio!*"

There was a young maiden named Rose
With erogenous zones in her toes.
    She remained onanistic
    Till a foot-fetishistic
Young man became one of her beaus.

Aubrey Beardsley

A naked young tart named Roselle
Walked the streets while ringing a bell;
When asked why she rang it
She answered, "Gol dang it!
Can't you see I have something to sell?"

There was a young lady of Rye
With a shape like a capital I.
When they said, "It's too bad,"
She learned how to pad;
Which shows you that figures can lie.

Edward Lear

S: *"There was a young girl from St. Cyr . . ."*

Aubrey Beardsley

There was a young girl from St. Cyr
Whose reflex reactions were queer.
  Her escort said, "Mabel
  Get up off the table;
That money's to pay for the beer."

From the depths of the crypt at St. Giles
Came a scream that resounded for miles.
  Said the vicar, "Good gracious!
  Has Father Ignatius
Forgotten the Bishop has piles?"

A young English woman named St. John
Met a red-skinned American In. John,
  Who made her his bride,
  And gave her beside
A dress with a gaudy bead Fr. John.

In the turbulent turgid St. Lawrence
Fell a luscious young damsel named Florence,
  Where poor famished fish
  Made this beautiful dish
An object of utter abhorrence.

There was a young girl from St. Paul
Wore a newspaper dress to a ball;
    But her dress caught on fire
    And burned her entire
Front page, sporting section, and all.

Said the venerable Dean of St. Paul's,
"Concerning them cracks in the walls—
    Do you think it would do
    If we filled them with glue?"
The Bishop of Lincoln said: "Balls!"[1]

A boy at Sault Ste. Marie
Said, "Spelling is all Greek to me,
    Till they learn to spell 'Soo'
    Without any 'u,'
Or an 'a' or an 'l' or a 't'!"

Three lovely young girls from St. Thomas
Attended dance-halls in pajamas.
    They were fondled all summer
    By sax, bass, and drummer—
I'm surprised that by now they're not mamas.

[1] Or:
There was a young man from St. Paul's
Who read *Harper's Bazaar* and *McCall's;*
    Till he grew such a passion
    For feminine fashion
That he knitted a snood for his balls.

There was a young curate of Salisbury
Whose manners were Halisbury-Scalisbury.
  He wandered round Hampshire
  Without any pampshire
Till the Vicar compelled him to Walisbury.[2]

There was an old couple in Sayville
Whose habits were quite medieval;
  They would strip to the skin
  Then each take a pin
And pick lint from the other one's navel.

A lady removing her scanties
Heard them crackle electrical chanties;
  Said her husband, "My dear,
  I very much fear
You suffer from amps in your panties."

A German explorer named Schlichter
Had a yen for a boa constrictor;
  When he lifted the tail,
  Achtung! 'Twas a male.
The constrictor, not Schlichter, was victor.

2. Included as the prime example of English English at its most frustrating: Salisbury used to be known as "Sarum"; Hampshire is familiarly called "Hants."

A waitress on day-shift at Schraffts
Has a couple of interesting craffts.
    She's exceedingly able
    At upsetting the table
And screwing in dumb-waiter schaffts.[3]

There was a young lady at sea
Who complained that it hurt her to pee.
    Said the brawny old mate,
    "That accounts for the state
Of the cook and the captain and me."

A Korean whose home was in Seoul
Had notions uncommonly droll;
    He'd get himself stewed
    And pose in the nude
On top of a telephone pole.

A contemptuous matron in Shoreham
Behaved with extreme indecorum.
    She snapped a sarcastic
    And secret elastic
Throughout the community forum.

3. H. Bate in the newsletter of The Poets' Club.

There once was a girl of Siam
Who said to her love, young Kiam,
   "If you take me, of course,
   You must do it by force,
But God knows you are stronger than I am."

From a tree hung a queer three-toed sloth,
Who to move was exceedingly wroth.
   But up in the tree
   He spied him a she
And combined the best features of both.

There was a young lady of Slough
Who said that she didn't know how.
   Then a young fellow caught her
   And jolly well taught her—
She lodges in Pimlico now.[4]

There was a young lady named Smith
Whose virtue was mostly a myth.
   She said, "Try as I can
   I can't find a man
Who it's fun to be virtuous with."[5]

4. "And so do a good many others of her kind," commented Norman Douglas.

5. Or:
There was a young writer named Smith
Whose virtue was largely a myth.
   We knew that he did it;
   He couldn't have hid it—
The question was only who with.

There once was a monarch of Spain
Who was terribly haughty and vain.
  When women were nigh
  He'd unbutton his fly
And have them with sneers of disdain.

There was a young man of high station
Who was found by a pious relation
  Making love in a ditch
  To—I won't say a bitch—
But a lady of *no* reputation.

There's a notable family named Stein,
There's Gertrude, there's Ep, and there's Ein.
  Gert's prose is the bunk,
  Ep's sculpture is junk,
And no one can understand Ein!

A bather whose clothing was strewed
By breezes that left her quite nude
  Saw a man come along,
  And, unless I am wrong,
You expected this line to be lewd.

Aubrey Beardsley

Aubrey Beardsley

A young schizophrenic named Struther
When told of the death of his mother,
    Said, "Yes, it's too bad,
    But I can't feel too sad,
After all, I *still* have each other."

A distinguished professor from Swarthmore
Had a date with a sexy young sophomore.
    As quick as a glance
    He stripped off his pants,
But he found that the sophomore'd got off more.

That exquisite bartender at Sweeney's
Is famed for his ale and free wienies;
    But I thought him uncouth
    To gulp gin and vermouth,
Chill the glasses, and piddle martinis.

Every time Lady Lowbodice swoons,
Her bubbies pop out like balloons;
    But her butler stands by
    With hauteur in his eye
And lifts them back in with warm spoons.

T: *"There was a young maid in Tahiti . . ."*

Aubrey Beardsley

There was a young maid in Tahiti
Whom the neighbors considered quite flahiti,
    For if Monday was fine
    She would hang on the line
An extremely diaphanous nahiti.

A forward young fellow named Tarr
Had a habit of goosing his Ma;
    "Go pester your sister,"
    She said when he kissed her,
"I've trouble enough with your Pa."

A young girl who was no good at tennis
But at swimming was really a menace,
    Took pains to explain,
    "It depends how you train;
I was a streetwalker in Venice."

A herder who hailed from Terre Haute
Fell in love with a young nanny goat;
    The daughter he sired
    Was greatly admired
For her beautiful angora coat.

A lady who lived by the Thames
Had a gorgeous collection of ghames;
    She had them reset
    In a large coronet
And a number of small diadhames.

There was a young woman of Thrace
Whose nose spread all over her face.
    She had very few kisses:
    The reason for this is
There wasn't a suitable place.

If intercourse gives you thrombosis
While continence causes neurosis,
    I prefer to expire
    Fulfilling desire
Than live on in a state of psychosis.

An old archeologist, Throstle,
Discovered a marvelous fossil.
    He knew from its bend
    And the knob on the end
'Twas the peter of Paul the Apostle.

A husband who lived in Tiberias
Once laughed himself nearly delirious;
    But he laughed at his wife
    Who took a sharp knife
With results that were quite deleterious.

Said a gleeful young man from Torquay,
"This is rather a red-letter day;
    For I've poisoned with sherbert
    My rich Uncle Herbert
Whose health *never* seemed to decay."

There was a young lady from Tottenham
Whose manners—well, she'd forgotten 'em.
    While at tea at the vicar's
    She kicked off her knickers
Explaining she felt much too hot in 'em.

"Far dearer to me than my treasure,"
The heiress declared, "is my leisure.
    For then I can screw
    The whole Harvard crew—
They're slow, but that lengthens the pleasure."

You will read in Professor Schmunk's treatise,
In the words of the famed Epictetus,
    The curious lore
    That young girls by the score
Are afflicted with athlete's foetus.

There once was a young man named Treet
Who minced as he walked down the street;
    He wore shoes of bright red
    And playfully said,
"I may not be strong, but I'm sweet."

A tone-deaf old person from Tring
When somebody asked him to sing,
    Replied, "It is odd
    But I cannot tell 'God
Save the Weasel' from 'Pop Goes the King.' "

A broken-down harlot named Tupps
Was heard to confess in her cups:
    "The height of my folly
    Was diddling a collie—
But I got a nice price for the pups."

André Domin

U: *"A man who was crude and uncouth . . ."*

1. But the prior of Dunstan St. Just,
Consumed with erotical lust,
    Raped the bishop's prize fowls
    (His treasured young owls)
And a little green lizard, what bust.

A man who was crude and uncouth
Met up with a maiden named Ruth
    But she gave him the air
    When he tried to betray 'er
One night in a telephone booth.

The Reverend Mr. Uprightly
Was cuckolded daily and nightly.
    He murmured, "Dear, dear!
    I would fain interfere,
If I knew how to do it politely."

A habit obscene and unsavory
Holds the Bishop of Wessex in slavery.
    With maniacal howls
    He deflowers young owls
Which he keeps in an underground aviary.[1]

A Kentucky-bound author named Vaughan,
Whose style often savored of scorn,
    Soon inscribed in his journals,
    "Here the corn's full of kernels,
And the Colonels are all full of corn."

A minister up in Vermont
Keeps a goldfish alive in the font;
    When he dips the babes in,
    It tickles their skin,
Which is all that the innocents want.

A widow whose singular vice
Was to keep her late husband on ice,
    Said, "It's been hard since I lost him—
    I'll never defrost him!
Cold comfort, but cheap at the price."

V: *"A Kentucky-bound author
named Vaughan . . ."*

W: *"There once was a Warden*

of Wadham . . ."

There once was a warden of Wadham
Who approved of the folkways of Sodom,
 For a man might, he said,
 Have a very poor head
But be a fine fellow, at bottom.

Said a foolish householder of Wales,
"An odor of coal gas prevails."
 She then struck a light,
 And later that night,
Was collected in seventeen pails.

There was a young lady of Wantage
Of whom the Town Clerk took advantage.
 Said the County Surveyor,
 "Of course you must pay her:
You've altered the line of her frontage."

There was a young lady of Waste
Who fled from a man in great haste.
        She fell as she fled
        And addled her head—
Sometimes she still dreams that she's chaste.

There was a young fellow named Weir
Who hadn't an atom of fear;
        He indulged a desire
        To touch a live wire—
Most any last line will do here.

As a girl soda-jerker, Miss West
Served soft drinks direct from the breast;
        The right yielded cherry,
        The left one strawberry,
Or Moxie, by special request.

A singular fellow of Weston
Has near fifty feet of intestine;
        Though a signal success
        In the medical press,
It isn't much good for digestin'.

Aubrey Beardsley

There was a young man of Westphalia
Who yearly got tail-ier and tail-ier,
    Till he took on the shape
    Of a Barbary ape
With the consequent paraphernalia.

There's an over-sexed lady named Whyte
Who insists on a dozen a night.
    A fellow named Cheddar
    Had the brashness to wed her—
His chance of survival is slight.

There was a young fellow named Willy
Who acted remarkably silly:
    At an All-Nations ball
    Dressed in nothing at all
He claimed that his costume was Chile.

A wanton young lady of Wimley,
Reproached for not acting more primly,
    Answered, "Heavens above!
    I know sex isn't love,
But it's such an attractive facsimile."

There was a young man from Wood's Hole
Who had an affair with a mole.
    Though a bit of a nancy
    He *did* like to fancy
Himself in the dominant role.

A sensitive lady from Worcester
At a ball met a fellow who gorcester;
    A lecherous guy
    With blood in his uy,
So she ducked out before he sedorcester.[1]

There was a young fellow named Wyatt
Who kept a big girl on the quiet;
    But down on the wharf
    He kept also a dwarf,
In case he should go on a diet.

There was a young lady named Wylde
Who kept herself quite undefiled
    By thinking of Jesus,
    Contagious diseases,
And the bother of having a child.

[1]. Or:
There was a young lady of Worcester
Who complained that too many men goosed her.
    So she traded her scanties
    For sandpaper panties.
Now they goose her much less than they used ter.

 X: *"There was a young sailor named Xavier . . ."*

There was a young sailor named Xavier,
Who cared not for God nor his Saviour:
    He walked on the decks
    Displaying his sex,
And was brigged for indecent behavior.

Y: *"There once was a baby of yore . . ."*

There once was a baby of yore
Whose parents found it a bore
　　And being afraid
　　It might be mislaid
They stored it away in a drawer.

An organist playing at York
Had a prick that could hold a small fork,
　　And between obligatos
　　He'd munch at tomatoes,
And keep up his strength while at work.

There was a young lady of Ypres
Who was shot in the ass by some snipers.
　　When she vented her air
　　Through the holes that were there
She confounded the Cameron Pipers.

A brainy professor named Zed
Dreamed one night of a buxom co-ed;
 He mussed and he bussed her
 And otherwise fussed her,
But the action was all in his head.

Z: *"A brainy professor named Zed . . ."*

There was a young lady of Zion
Looked around for a shoulder to cry on;
 So she married a spouse
 From a very old house
And started to cry on the scion.

PART THREE:

THE LITERATURE OF THE LIMERICK

Edward Lear

Aubrey Beardsley

The editor would like, first, to express his gratitude to the able and gracious staffs of many libraries, in particular those of the Beinecke Rare Book and Manuscript Library at Yale University, the Library of Congress at Washington, D. C., and the New York Public Library.

Many friends, friends of friends and valued business associates in the greater New York metropolitan area and elsewhere have made contributions of one kind or another. Among them are Mrs. Joan T. Allen; John Allison of Pound Ridge; David W. Ballard of Pound Ridge; Amos Bethke of Briarcliff Manor; Herbert Brean; Doris Coffin; Sheldon Cotler of Scarsdale; David J. Coveney of Philadelphia, Pennsylvania; Noble D. ("Red") Dougherty; H. Carlyle Estes of Cos Cob, Connecticut; Peter Forstenzer; Martin Gardner of Hastings-on-Hudson; Ben Hall; Martin Kaiden; Michael E. Keene; Edgar H. Lawrence; Everett B. Laybourne of Los Angeles; Walter C. Lefmann; Jerome E. Light, D.D.S., of Armonk; Harlan Logan of Meriden, New Hampshire; Professor J. Bard McNulty of Trinity College, Hartford, Connecticut; J. Bruce McWilliams of Pound Ridge; Stewart M. Ogilvy; Royal Peterson and John Poillon, both of Philadelphia, Pennsylvania; Michael Sasanoff of Silvermine, Connecticut; Bernard Simon of London, England; Halbert F. Speer; Professor T. J. Spencer of Washington, D. C.; Thomas L. Stix, Sr.; Kelso F. Sutton; Lewis Titterton of Pound Ridge; Herbert Tolmach, D.D.S., of Pound Ridge; George G. Tyler; Walter Weir and Julian Wolff, M.D.

And very special thanks to that genial and informed gentleman, Carleton Holmes Davis of Old Lyme, Connecticut, who opened his files, his library and his mind to your editor. And to ·Robert C. Gordon, Advertising Director of *Time,* The Weekly Newsmagazine, who brought the two of us together.

The library of limerology which follows is divided into two sections. The first section consists of those books which are available only in libraries—and sometimes not in libraries. The second section is a listing of those books of limericks (many of them out of print) which may still be obtainable through bookstores and other dealers by any reader interested in building up his own collection. Happy hunting!

WILLIAM S. BARING-GOULD

"Stonycroft"
Pound Ridge, New York
September 3, 1966

The History of Sixteen Wonderful Old Women. London: John Harris, 1821.

The earliest known book of limericks.

Anecdotes and Adventures of Fifteen Gentlemen. London: John Marshall, 1822.

LELAND, CHARLES GODFREY. *Ye Book of Copperheads* Philadelphia: Leypoldt, 1863.

"L. L. D." [CHARLES GODFREY LELAND?] *Spirit of the Times.* 1863.

The New Book of Nonsense. Philadelphia: The Sanitary Commission of the Great Central Fair, 1864.

Ye Book of Bubbles. Philadelphia: The Sanitary Commission of the Great Central Fair, 1864.

Inklings for Thinklings. Philadelphia: The Sanitary Commission of the Great Central Fair, 1864.

A New Book of Nonsense. London, 1868.

Only a reference to the title of this book has survived. It is supposed to be the earliest known collection of erotic limericks.

Cythera's Hymnal, or Flakes from the Foreskin: A Col-lection of Songs, Poems, Nursery Rhymes, Quiddities, etc. "Oxford." [London, 1870] Printed at the University Press for the Society for Promoting Useful Knowledge."

Contains fifty-one erotic limericks titled "Nursery Rhymes." See comment in main text.

Light Green. Cambridge University, 1872.

A burlesque magazine of which two numbers were issued.

The Pearl: A Monthly Journal of Facetiae and Voluptuous Reading. "Oxford: Printed at the University Press." [London: Cameron, 1879-80].

According to Gershon Legman, there were eighteen monthly issues, from July, 1879, through December, 1880, the first six containing 61 (of 65) limericks, titled "Nursery Rhymes." There is supposed to exist an American reprint, published *circa* 1932 in which all issues are erroneously dated 1880: "London: Printed for the Society of Vice, 1880."

The Cremorne: A Magazine of Wit, Facetiae, Parody, Graphic Tales of Love, etc. London: Privately printed [Cameron], "1851" [1882].
A sequel to *The Pearl.* The first issue, August, 1882, was dated "January, 1851." Issue no. 3 ("March, 1851") contained five limericks.

AIKEN, CONRAD, *A Seizure of Limericks*. London: W. H. Allen, 1965.

ANDERSON, C. V. J. (ed.). *Forbidden Limericks*. San Francisco: Logos Books, n. d.

"With sickening drawings by Pablo Kamastra."

The Bagman's Book of Limericks. Paris: Excel Books, n. d.

Two hundred and fifty-two erotic limericks, in English, mostly from Douglas and Legman.

BARING-GOULD, WILLIAM S. and DONOVAN, DAVID. *Fifty Famous Limericks*. Minneapolis, Minnesota: Privately printed, 1934.

Limericks popular among the students and faculty members of the University of Minnesota in the year it was mimeographed, 1934.

————. *Fifty More Famous Limericks*. Minneapolis, Minnesota: Privately printed, 1935.

A second serving of the same.

BEILENSON, PETER (ed.). *Peter Pauper's Limerick Book*. Mount Vernon, New York: Peter Pauper Press, 1940.

"Dedicated to the memory of those we did not dare print." Three hundred and thirty-one limericks, illustrated by Herb Roth.

BISHOP, MORRIS. "On the Limerick," *The New York Times Book Review,* January 3, 1965.

————. *Spilt Milk*. New York: G. P. Putnam's Sons, 1942.

A collection of Mr. Bishop's light verse, including twenty-nine superb limericks, illustrated by Richard Taylor.

BOMBAUGH, C. C. *Oddities and Curiosities of Words and Literature,* ed. and annotator MARTIN GARDNER. New York: Dover Publications, Inc., 1961.

"This new edition . . . is an unabridged and unaltered republication of the first 310 pages and the chapters of Refractory Rhymings and Conformity of Sense to Sound of Gleanings for the Curious from the Harvest-fields of Literature, third edition, published in 1890 by J. B. Lippincott Company."

BRAYBROOKE, PATRICK, F.R.S.L. *Some Celebrities in Verse*. London: The C. W. Daniel Company, 1930.

Foreword by Max Pemberton.

BROCK, H. I. "A Century of Limericks," *The New York Times Magazine,* November 17, 1946.

————. *The Little Book of Limericks*. New York: Duell, Sloan and Pearce, 1947.

One of the best of the modern books of limericks, all nursery-clean. The idea of the collection, Mr. Brock writes in his dedication, was given to him by Lester Markel, Sunday Editor of *The New York Times*. The beginning was the article cited above.

BYRON, WARD (ed.). *The Poets.* New York: The Poets Club.

The more-or-less monthly newsletter of The Poets Club.

CERF, BENNETT (ed.). *Out on a Limerick.* New York: Harper & Brothers, 1960.

"A collection of over 300 of the world's best printable limericks assembled, revised, dry-cleaned and annotated by Mister Cerf. With illustrations by Saxon." About one-third of the limericks in this volume were reprinted from the compiler's "Cerfboard" column in *This Week Magazine.*

Cleopatra's Scrapbook. "Blue Grass, Kentucky" [Wheeling, West Virginia?], 1928.

A source cited by Legman.

CORNISH, KENNETH. *Nonsense Verse.* Durban, South Africa: Knox Printing and Publishing Company, 1948.

Foreword by A. B. Hughes, editor of *The Sunday Express.* Illustrated by Leyden. Limericks about the improbable places which enliven the map of South Africa.

CRISP, QUENTIN. *All This and Bevin Too.* London: Nicholson & Watson, 1943.

Illustrated by Mervyn Peake. A limerick sequence of forty-eight verses.

[DAVIES, RANDALL ROBERT HENRY]. *A Little More Nonsense.* Kensington: The Cayme Press, 1923.

Illustrated with woodcuts from a specimen book published in 1862.

———. *A Lytell Book of Nonsense.* Kensington: The Cayme Press, 1925.

Illustrated with woodcuts from fifteenth and sixteenth-century books.

———. *Less Eminent Victorians.* London: Peter Davies, 1927.

Illustrated with woodcuts.

DOUGLAS, NORMAN. *Some Limericks.* [Florence: G. Orioli]. Privately printed, 1928.

"Collected for the use of Students, & ensplendour'd with Introduction, Geographical Index, and with Notes explanatory and critical. . ." "This edition is issued to Subscribers only. It consists of one hundred and ten copies, numbered and signed by the Author, numbers 1-10 being on special paper priced at ten guineas each, and numbers 11-110 at five guineas each. The price of both sets will be doubled after January 31, 1929. The type has been distributed. This copy is No. [numbered and signed in ink]." Bound in rough gold linen. Five later editions cited in Legman's *The Limerick.*

[DRAKE]. *A Book of Anglo-Saxon Verse.* "Nantucket" [Oakland, California]: 1949. "Printed on the Concavo-Convex Press in Racine."

"Newly arranged and edited. With notes by various hands." Unbound sheets. One hundred and sixty-one erotic limericks, with an Index of Rimes. One of the sources used by Legman in compiling *The Limerick.*

DULAC, EDMUND. *Lyrics Pathetic and Humourous from A to Z.* London: Frederick Warne & Co., 1908.

Illustrated by the author.

Eros (eds.). "Bawdy Limericks: The Folklore of the Intellectual." Vol. I, No. 4 (Winter, 1962).

EUWER, ANTHONY. *The Limeratomy.* New York: James B. Pond, 1917.

"A Compendium of Universal Knowledge for the More Perfect Understanding of the Human Machine Done in the Limerick Tongue and Copiously Visualized with Illustragraphs by the Perpetrator."

FADIMAN, CLIFTON. "There Was an Old Man of Tobago." In *Any Number Can Play.* Cleveland and New York: The World Publishing Company, 1957.

"FALMOUTH, JOHN" (ed.). *Ninety-five Limericks.* Suffern, New York: Limerick Press, 1932.

"A contribution to the folklore of our time." Publicly published with erotic terms expurgated with XXX's, restored in the edition listed here. All but

fifteen of the limericks are from Douglas and *Immortalia.*

Farmer Gray. [Overseas? U.S. Marine Aircraft Group 94, *circa* 1945.]

Nine mimeographed pages, seventy limericks. Another of the sources cited by Legman.

From Bed to Verse.

"An unabashed anthology; being a collection af [*sic*] the world's best-loved feelthy limericks collected . . . by divers idle hands for the amusement and delectation of some members of the Army of Occupation in Germany and their friends. Germany, very privately printed, 1945." "Acknowledgment is made to Norman Douglas, in whose *Some Limericks* . . . many of the verses were previously collected." "Limited to one hundred and fifty copies, unnumbered and unsigned by the editors."

GARDINER, FLORENCE HERRICK (ed.). *Limericks.* Philadelphia: J. B. Lippincott Company, 1921.

Glad to Obscene You.

"By Mr. Anon, Poet Emeritus and Merry Tous." Unpublished collection. One of the many items lent to the editor by Mr. Carleton Holmes Davis.

GORDON, GEORGE AND EISENBERG, LAWRENCE. *Limericks for the John.* New York: Kanrom Inc., 1963.

GOREY, EDWARD. *The Listing Attic.* New York: Duell,

Sloan and Pearce; Boston: Little, Brown and Company, 1954.

Sixty limericks with drawings by the talented Mr. Gorey. "The limericks are in neither the Lear nor in the anonymous tradition, by which last is meant that none of them are [*sic*] obscene. The majority are macabre, some are nearly pointless, and five are written in what the unwary may take to be French."

Grand Prix Limerix: 1,001 New Limericks You Never Saw Before! Fort Worth, Texas: SRI Publishing Company, 1966.

The author is reputed to be the San Francisco advertising executive, John Coulthard.

GRAVES, G. L. "The Cult of the Limerick." *The Cornhill Magazine,* Vol. XLIV, No. 260 (February, 1948).

HALE, SUSAN (ed.). *Nonsense Book: A Collection of Limericks.* Boston: Marshall Jones, 1919.

Illustrated by the editor.

"HALL, J. MORTIMER." *Anecdota Americana.* "Boston" [New York: Printed by Guy d'Isère for David Moss, 1927].

"Explicitly, an anthology of tales in the vernacular. Elucidatory Preface by J. Mortimer Hall. Anecdotes collected and taken down by William Passemon. Pen and ink drawings by Anton Erdman. Woodblocks drawn & cut by Bruce MacAile. Printed and published by Humphrey Adams for the Association of Hypocrites, solely on subscription of its members." Reprinted New York, 1928? with an extra poem. Expurgated edition New York, 1933. Reprinted, omitting the Preface, 1934. Revised as *The New Anecdota America,* New York, 1934.

"HARDE, DICK" (ed.). *Lusty Limericks & Bawdy Ballads.*

A mimeographed collection, with no place of publication, publisher or date of publication given.

[HARRISON]. MS., New York, 1947.

A general collection including fifty limericks, probably original, not found elsewhere. Another of the sources used by Legman in compiling *The Limerick.*

Heated Limericks. "Paris" [Havana]: Privately printed for Erotica Biblion Society, 1933.

Cited by Legman as "Not seen. Possibly a reprint of 'Falmouth' or Douglas."

Hurler avec les Loups.

A privately printed edition of fifty-eight (mostly familiar) limericks. No compiler's name, publisher, place of publication or date of publication given. Listed here because it is a choice example of the bookmaker's art. Perhaps a product of America's Amateur Press Association?

Index Limericus. MS., Berkeley, California, 1941-47.

Referred to by Legman as a "Card index, including all the limericks in *Immortalia,* Douglas, 'Falmouth,' *Pornographia Literaria, That Immortal Garland,*

Unexpurgated, and *Farmer Gray,* with 330 new examples from the transactions of the American Limerick Society, in Berkeley, 1942-47."

Investigation into the Epistemology and Classification of Limericks, An. [Rochester, New York: U. S. Army Medical Corps, 1943.]

Cited by Legman as "A small but spirited collection" (mimeographed).

JACKSON, HOLBROOK (ed.). *The Complete Nonsense of Edward Lear.* New York: Dover Publications, Inc., 1951.

"JONES, DAVE E." *A Collection of sea songs and ditties . . . .* [U. S., *circa* 1928.]

Legman writes: "Mostly ballads, including eleven limericks. Hole for padlock through outer edges of pages and canvas wrapper."

LA BARRE, WESTON. "The Psychopathology of Drinking Songs," *Psychiatry* (Washington, D. C.) May, 1939.

Lapses in Limerick. MS., Ann Arbor, Michigan, 1935-38.

Another of the sources cited by Legman: "Includes all the limericks in *The Pearl, Immortalia,* Douglas, 'Falmouth,' and *Anecdota Americana* II, with 350 examples orally collected—'all metrically perfect' [*n. b.*]. Quoted here from the partial revision, N. Y., 1941."

Laundered Limericks. Mount Vernon, New York: The Peter Pauper Press, 1960.

Illustrated by Henry R. Martin.

LEGMAN, GERSHON [originally GEORGE ALEXANDER]. "The Limerick: A History in Brief." *The Horn Book: Studies in Erotic Folklore and Bibliography.* New Hyde Park, New York: University Books Inc., 1964.

———. *The Limerick: 1700 Examples, with Notes, Variants, and Index.* Paris: Hautes Études, 1953.

See description in our main text.

"Limerick Addenda." *The New York Times Magazine,* December 8, 1946.

Limericks.

A Dittoed collection of 160 bawdy limericks, mostly familiar, grouped into twelve Chapters and an Appendix. As in most collections of this kind, no compiler's name, place or date of publication is given.

Little Limerick Book: (An Uncensored Collection). Mount Vernon, New York: The Peter Pauper Press, 1955.

Illustrated by Henry R. Martin.

McCORD, DAVID (ed.). *What Cheer!: An Anthology of American and British Humorous and Witty Verse Gathered, Sifted, and Salted, with an Introduction by David McCord.* New York: Coward-McCann Inc., 1945.

Editor McCord devotes one full chapter to limericks, presenting thirty-seven examples.

[McINTYRE, C. F.]. *That Immortal Garland.* MS., Berkeley, California, 1942.

"Being a collection of previously unpublished limericks from the literary remains of my uncle, who gave me permission to offer them ten years after his death. From the Sign of the Lampadophore, 1941." Introduction signed, "Norman Douglas, Amalfi, 1917." "Apology of the Executor," dated 1942. One hundred and six original limericks. With excurses to the first sixty, Index, and Bibliography in the manner of Douglas. One of the sources used by Legman in compiling *The Limerick*.

[MORSE, A. REYNOLDS]. *Immortalia*. [Philadelphia], 1927.

"An anthology of American ballads, sailors' songs, cowboy songs, college songs, parodies, limericks, and other humorous verses and doggerel now for the first time brought together in book form. By A Gentleman About Town. One thousand copies . . . privately printed for subscribers. None is for general sale." One hundred and three limericks, much poorer in quality than the rest of the collection. Reprinted by offset, New York, *circa* 1932.

————. *The Limerick: A Facet of Our Culture*. "Mexico City: The Cruciform Press" [Cleveland?], 1944.

"A study of the history and development of the limerick, ensplendor'd with over two hundred examples of the immortal verse form, commentaries, and index. ANNOTATED and UNEXPURGATED. Privately printed for private circulation to subscribers only; no copies for general sale. *The Limerick* has been printed for a small number of Experts and Specialists, Scholars, Psychiatrists, Sociologists and Anthropologists. The project has been conceived, executed, and concluded as a tribute to our lost freedom—the freedom of the individual. It is dedicated to Man's renaissance from the blind tyranny of Law. Two Hundred and Fifty copies have been manufactured . . . Each is numbered."

MUMFORD, ETHEL WATTS (ed.). *The Limerick Up to Date Book*. San Francisco: Paul Elder and Company, 1903.

Illustrated by Ethel Watts Mumford and Addison Mizner.

NASH, OGDEN. *The Pocket Book of Ogden Nash*. New York: Pocket Books, Inc. (Cardinal Edition), 1962.

Mr. Nash's marvelous limericks are scattered throughout his many collections of light verse, and the reader is invited to have fun finding them. This is, however, a good place to start.

"NOSTI." *A Collection of Limericks*. Switzerland, 1944.

See reference in main text.

PARKES, HARRY. *Random Rhymes*. London: Frederick Warne & Company, 188?.

Poems, Ballads, and Parodies. [Detroit: McClurg?, *circa* 1928.]

A volume of collected verse hitherto unpublished. "Benares—Paris: Published for distribution among members only, and not for sale, by Benardin Society, 1923." Includes ten limericks. Another of the sources cited by Legman.

Pornographia Literaria. [U. S., *circa* 1941.]

"In spite of the similar number of limericks," says Legman, "an entirely different collection from Douglas."

The Raunchy Reader. Fort Worth, Texas: SRI Publishing Company, 1965.

REED, (HERBERT) LANGFORD. *The Complete Limerick Book.* New York and London: G. P. Putnam's Sons, 1925.

"The origin, history and achievements of the limerick, with over 400 selected examples." With twenty-four illustrations by H. M. Bateman.

——— (ed.). *Mr. Punch's Limerick Book.* London: Cobden-Sanderson, 1934.

Foreword by A. P. Herbert. Illustrated by G. S. Sherwood.

———. *My Limerick Book.* London: Thomas Nelson and Sons, Ltd., 1937.

Illustrated by Joyce Dennys.

———. *The New Limerick Book.* London: Herbert Jenkins Limited, 1937.

With forty illustrations by Batchelor.

"SCHWEINICKLE, O. U." *The Book of a Thousand Laughs.* [Wheeling, West Virginia?, 1928.]

One of the sources cited by Legman.

The Smile on the Face of the Tiger. Boston: Bacon & Brown, 1908.

Songs My Mother Never Taught Me. [New York: Pershing Rifles, City College, 1944.]

Still another of the sources used by Legman in compiling *The Limerick.*

THORNLEY, THOMAS. *Provocative Verse and Libellous Limericks.* Cambridge: W. Heffer & Sons Ltd., 1936.

Unexpurgated. Bidet Press [Los Angeles, 1943.]

Says Legman: "169 limericks, followed by 'Socially Conscious Pornography,' a limerick-sequence in fifteen stanzas and chorus. . . . Reprinted without title: 'Edited by R. Schloch, Ph.D.' The Open Box Press [California, *ante* 1951]."

UNTERMEYER, LOUIS. "Good Old Limericks." *Good Housekeeping,* December, 1945.

——— (ed.). *Lots of Limericks: Light, Lusty, and Lasting.* Garden City, New York: Doubleday & Co., Inc.

Poet Untermeyer brings together 263 limericks, some "Slightly Ridiculous," some "Lightly Amatory," some "Rollicking and Rowdy," with an Introduction on "The Limerick, Its Life and High Times" and many delicious drawings by Richard Taylor.

URDA, NICK. *Eighty-Eight Best Limericks.* Herrick Center, Pennsylvania, 1964.

VAUGHAN, STANTON (ed.). *700 Limerick Lyrics: A Collection of Choice Humorous Versifications.* New York: T. J. Carey and Company, 1904.

Not by any means all of the "700" are limericks but doggerel newspaper poetry of the early Twentieth Century variety.

"VICARION, Count PALMIRO" [CHRISTOPHER LOGUE]. *Book of Limericks.* Paris, 1955.

See comment in main text.

"VOX, CAROL" [WILLIAM HOUGHTON SPRAGUE]. *The Sphinx and the Mummy: A Book of Limericks.* New York and Boston: H. M. Caldwell Company, 1909.

Illustrated by H. Boylston Dummer.

WASHBURN, WILLIAM LEWIS. *A Bouquet of Choice Limericks Garnished from Various Sources and Printed for the Edification & Amusement of Lovers of This Form of Verse.* Audubon, New Jersey: The Palmetto Press, [1935?].

WATERMAN, PAUL. *Those Brats from Limerick.* Dexter, Missouri: Candor Press, 1964.

WELLS, CAROLYN (ed.). *Book of American Limericks.* New York and London: G. P. Putnam's Sons, 1925.

————. *The Book of Humorous Verse.* New York: Halcyon House, 1941.

————. *A Nonsense Anthology.* New York: Dover Publications, Inc., 1958.

————. *A Whimsey Anthology.* New York: Dover Publications, Inc., 1953.

Originally published by Charles Scribner's Sons in 1906.

[WOOD, CLEMENT]. *The Facts of Life—in Limericks.* [Delanson, New York, 1943.]

With a Preface by "Richard Offenbach Harder, Ph.D." Ninety-two limericks, arranged by subjects, erotologically classified.

WHITE, ALISON. "With Birds in His Beard." *The Saturday Review,* January 15, 1966.

An article on Edward Lear, the Founding Father.

WILLIAMS, OSCAR (ed.). *The Silver Treasury of Light Verse from Geoffrey Chaucer to Ogden Nash.* New York: The New American Library (Mentor Edition), 1957.

Mr. Williams has sprinkled limericks, many of them of recent composition, through the 408 pages of his text.

"WITHERSPOON, SHAEMAS J. A." *The Glimerick Book.* New York: The Glimerick Publishing Company, 1945.

"Containing New and Original Glimericks or Mystifying Limericks Together with Some of the Author's Old Classics Made into Glimericks." Illustrated by Ann Nooney.

The World's Best Limericks. Mount Vernon, New York: The Peter Pauper Press, 1951.

One hundred and ninety-two limericks, illustrated by Richard Floethe.

Yale Tales. [Pittsfield, Massachusetts, 1952.]

Mimeographed. Eighty limericks, about fifteen new, followed by "The Good Ship *Venus.*"